SG24-5754-00

IBM

International Technical Support Organization

Design and Implement Servlets, JSPs, and EJBs for IBM WebSphere Application Server

August 2000

D1484848

Take Note!

Before using this information and the product it supports, be sure to read the general information in Appendix A, "Special notices" on page 179.

First Edition (August 2000)

This edition applies to Version 3.02 of WebSphere Application Server and VisualAge for Java for use with the Windows NT Operating System.

Comments may be addressed to:
IBM Corporation, International Technical Support Organization
Dept. QXXE Building 80-E2
650 Harry Road
San Jose, California 95120-6099

Contents

Figures

Tables

Preface

This IBM Redbook provides design guidelines for developing e-business applications based on servlets, JavaServer Pages (JSP) and Enterprise JavaBean (EJB) technologies.

The guidelines are based on WebSphere Application Server Advanced Edition. The redbook describes the concepts of workload balancing through the use of a network dispatcher and clones of the Application Server.

This book proposes a design of Web applications based on design patterns, such as the model-view-controller paradigm and the command framework. In this context, the usage of enterprise beans, including access beans, associations, and collections is explored in detail, and a set of EJB-based design patterns is described.

Part 1, "Choosing appropriate Web technologies" of this redbook provides guidelines on how to design specific components of an application. It also explains why and when a designer should move business logic from JavaBeans to a more powerful technology like Enterprise JavaBeans. By doing so, we explain what important aspects of the technology must be taken into account.

Part 2, "Design patterns and guidelines" is a set of design patterns for building e-business applications. Readers can use the information directly from a chapter and apply it in their own designs.

The team that wrote this redbook

This redbook was produced by a team of specialists from around the world working at the International Technical Support Organization San Jose Center.

Joaquin Picon is a consultant at the International Technical Support Organization, San Jose Center. He writes extensively and teaches IBM classes worldwide on application development, object technology, CORBA and Enterprise JavaBeans. Before joining the ITSO, Joaquin worked at the IBM Application Enabling Center Of Competency in France. Joaquin holds a degree in telecommunications from the Institut National de Telecommunications.

Regis Coqueret is an IT specialist at the EMEA WebSphere Technical Sales Center in La Gaude, France. Working first in the French steel industry's Information Technology, he has been involved in object technology, Smalltalk, then Java since 1990. He has five years of experience in development of application development programming tools in the IBM Paris laboratory, and two years of experience in technical support on Java, Web technologies and Enterprise JavaBeans. He holds an engineering degree from the Ecole des Mines de Paris and the Institut Superieur d'Informatique et d'Automatique.

Andreas Hutfless is an Advisory IT Architect in Germany. He has seven years of experience in Information Technology and four years of experience in the Web and Java. Andreas holds a degree in computer science from the University of Bonn. He has worked at IBM for three years. His areas of expertise include Java, Internet technologies and protocols, Enterprise JavaBeans and Linux.

Gopal Indurkhya is a Tech Lead in E-Commerce division at First Union National Bank, Charlotte, North Carolina. He has 15 years of experience in Information Technology, which includes 10 years of experience in object technology in C++ and Java. He holds a master degree in Mechanical Engineering from IIT, Kanpur, India, and a master degree in Manufacturing Systems Engineering from the University of Nebraska, Lincoln, Nebraska. His areas of expertise include Internet technologies, Enterprise JavaBeans and Neural Networks.

Martin Weiss is an Advisory IT Specialist in Switzerland. He has been with IBM since 1978, working in application development (IBM mainframe, AS/400, OS/2, Windows NT). Since 1993 he has been focusing on object technology as a developer and mentor in VisualAge customer projects (Smalltalk, C++, Java). He has sound experience in developing Java Enterprise applications for IBM WebSphere Application Servers. He is co-author of the IBM Redbook *Enterprise JavaBeans Development Using VisualAge for Java*, SG24-5429.

Thanks to the following people for their invaluable contributions to this project:

Ueli Wahli
Yvonne Lyon
Gabrielle Velez
ITSO, San Jose

Kyle Brown
Steven Waleski
Scott Rich
Lucy Barnhill
Ritchie Schacher
Guru Vasudeva
IBM, Raleigh

Graeme Dixon
Keys Botzum
Amber Roy-Chowdbury
Chriss Stephens
Transarc lab, Pittsburgh

Joe Bockhold
IBM, Rochester

George Copeland
Michael Conner
Geoffrey Hambrick
Greg Truty
IBM, Austin

Leonard Theivendra
Teresa Kan
Arthur Ryman
IBM, Toronto

Thomas Alcott
WebSphere Worldwide Tech Sales Support

Kevin J. Williams
IBM, Boulder

Jonathan Adams
Anthony Griffin
Joe Parman
IBM Hursley, Pattern Development Kit

Comments welcome

Your comments are important to us!

We want our Redbooks to be as helpful as possible. Please send us your comments about this or other Redbooks in one of the following ways:

- Fax the evaluation form found in "IBM Redbooks review" on page 201 to the fax number shown on the form.

- Use the online evaluation form found at `http://www.redbooks.ibm.com/`

- Send your comments in an Internet note to `redbook@us.ibm.com`

Part 1. Choosing appropriate Web technologies

Part 1 of this redbook describes a number of Web technologies and gives guidelines about the structure of Web server applications.

We describe a topology based on:

- WebSphere Application Server
- Application Server clones
- Servlet load balancing
- WebSphere Performance Pack with the Network Dispatcher

To structure a Web application we describe concepts and give guidelines on:

- Servlets and JavaServer Pages
- Command framework
- Enterprise beans based on the EJB specification and extensions such as:
  - Access beans
  - Associations
  - Collections

1

Chapter 1. Introduction

Figure 1 shows a broad view of what we attempt to cover in this book. The main focus is to provide design guidelines or *best practices* about designing an e-business application that will be deployed on IBM WebSphere Advanced Edition.

The main technologies used in this redbook for designing e-business applications are:

- Servlets
- JavaServer Pages (JSP)
- Enterprise JavaBeans (EJB)

The applications may interact with other external systems, such as:

- Tier 1 and Tier 0 devices
- Directory and Security services (LDAP)
- Other e-business applications following a business-to-business model

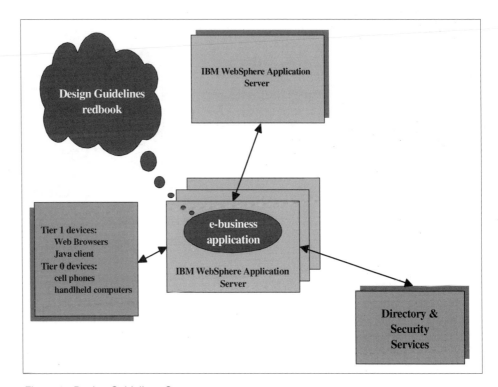

Figure 1. Design Guidelines Scope

References to other redbooks

This book can be considered as a supplement to the books listed here. So, before starting with this book, we recommend reading two additional books:

- *Servlet and JSP Programming with IBM WebSphere Studio and VisualAge for Java*, SG24 5755

- *Patterns for e-business: User-to-Business Patterns for Topology 1 and 2 using WebSphere Advanced Edition*, SG24-5864

A scalable and reliable technology

We start by defining a reference topology that serves as the basis for developing scalable and reliable e-business applications. The main functions that contribute to creating this topology are described in Chapter 2, "A scalable and reliable topology" on page 7. We analyze how applications, relying on a Model-View-Controller general pattern, receive benefits from some of our design patterns. Figure 2 represents the foundation of this redbook.

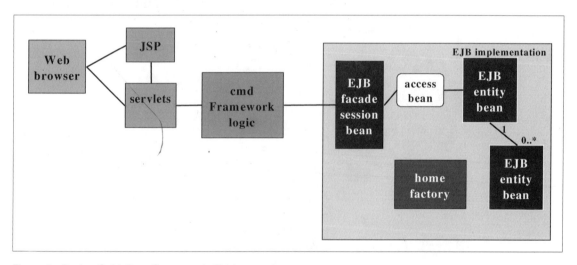

Figure 2. Design Guidelines Components Environment

Pervasive computing

This starting point gives a widespread scenario based on a Web browser client talking to a combination of servlets, JSPs, and JavaBeans encapsulating business logic. As new devices like cell phones or handheld computers become more and more common, applications must be designed to support these devices. Chapter 3, "Support for pervasive computing" on page 17 describes how to make the design of servlets controller flexible enough to accommodate existing or yet to be invented disparate devices.

Command framework

The granularity of artifacts on the server (for example, objects, tables, procedure calls, and files) often causes a single client-initiated business logic request to involve several round-trip messages between the client and server. This may include several calls to perform the business task and then several more calls to retrieve the results of that task.

There are several possible styles for how business logic can be implemented, including EJB, JDBC direct database access, JDBC access to stored procedures, the Common Connector Framework, file system access, and so on. In addition to different implementation programming models, each of these styles has a different way to invoke a request to execute business logic. Chapter 4, "WebSphere command framework" on page 23 describes a generic framework, that can potentially handle multiple protocols to accommodate any target server objects.

Enterprise JavaBeans

The next step after deciding to use the command framework is to choose how to implement the business logic. As proponents for the Enterprise JavaBeans technology, in Chapter 5, "The need for EJB technology" on page 45, we attempt to give some good reasons for encapsulating the business logic as enterprise beans.

Access beans

When you program directly to the enterprise bean interfaces, you increase the complexity of your user program and can incur significant performance problems. Each call to the enterprise proxy object is a remote call, so accessing a large number of entity bean attributes can take a significant amount of time. These problems, however, are now largely solved by the use of access beans. Chapter 6, "Access beans" on page 51 describes access beans and explains why we use them between the facade and entity beans.

Associations

Associations are relationships between concepts that indicate some meaningful connection. The Enterprise JavaBeans specification has concealed this subject. Fortunately, VisualAge for Java and IBM WebSphere Advanced Edition provide enterprise beans associations support. However, the generated code for associations may not always fulfill your requirements. The purpose of Chapter 7, "Associations" on page 61 is to give important additional information when using associations.

Collections

Chapter 8, "Collections" on page 101 addresses the problem of handling collections of objects. For that purpose, the Enterprise JavaBeans specification defines finders. How finders are executed by the IBM WebSphere Advanced Edition application server is explained in this chapter.

Design patterns

In Part 2, "Design patterns and guidelines" on page 121, we discuss some design issues presented as design patterns. If you want to follow the logical flow in Figure 2, from left to the right, you can read the facade pattern described in 10.2, "EJB session facade to entity beans" on page 157. The facade provides various use-case-oriented services to clients.

Chapter 2. A scalable and reliable topology

This redbook discusses design guidelines based on a given reference topology. To render a scalable and reliable system that is able to accommodate most large scale e-business applications with the best performance, our topology relies on several IBM products:

- IBM WebSphere Advanced Edition
- DB2
- Network Dispatcher
- IBM HTTP Server
- IBM SecureWay

Figure 3 has combined all of these products in the following topology.

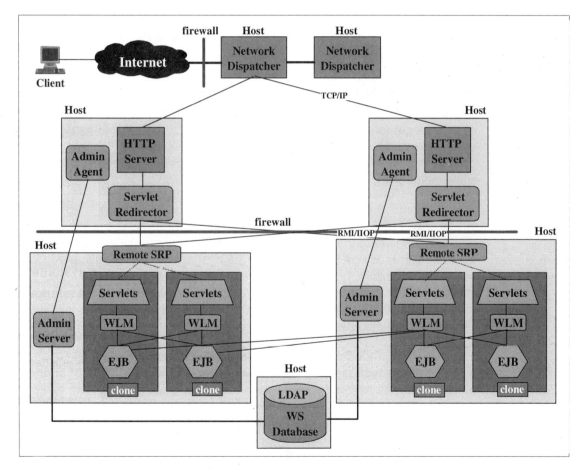

Figure 3. Reference Topology

The goal of the reference topology is to introduce the elements which participate in providing scalability, reliability and performance. Variations to the topology are not discussed. Several different choices can be made, such as separate clones for servlets and enterprise beans, which can run on different machines. However, variations to our topology are not discussed.

Our reference topology is further explained throughout this chapter.

2.1 TCP/IP load balancing and failover

IBM SecureWay Network Dispatcher is the load balancing component of IBM WebSphere Performance Pack, and addresses stability availability and critical load issues. It consists of three functions: the Dispatcher, Interactive Session Support (ISS) and the new Content Based Routing (CBR) function. These three functions can be deployed separately or together.

For any detailed information, refer to *IBM WebSphere Performance Pack: Load Balancing with IBM SecureWay Network Dispatcher*, SG24-5858.

2.1.1 How the Dispatcher works

The Dispatcher creates the illusion of having just one server by grouping systems together into a *cluster* that behaves as a single, virtual server. The service provided is no longer tied to a specific server system, so you can add or remove systems from the cluster, or shut down systems for maintenance, while maintaining continuous service for your clients.

For the clients, the balanced traffic among servers seems to be a single, virtual server, and the site appears as a single IP address to the world. All requests are sent to the IP address of the Dispatcher machine, which decides for each client request which server is the best one to accept requests, according to certain dynamically set weights. The Dispatcher routes the client's request to the selected server, and then the server responds directly to the client without any further involvement of the Dispatcher. The Dispatcher can also detect a failed server and route traffic around it.

The Dispatcher receives the packets sent to the cluster. These packets have a source and a destination address; the destination address is the IP address of the cluster. All servers in the cluster and in the Dispatcher system have their own IP address and an alias for the IP address of the cluster; the Dispatcher system has the cluster address aliased on the network interface, while all the TCP servers that will be load balanced by this ND machine have the cluster address aliased on the loopback adapter. The Dispatcher system checks which server is the next best server to handle the load and routes the packet to that server. The Dispatcher routes this request based on the hardware address of the network adapter (MAC address) of the chosen server. It changes the hardware address of the packet to the hardware address of the selected server and sends the packet to the server. However, the Dispatcher does not change the source and destination IP addresses in the packet. The server receives the packet and accepts it, because all servers in the cluster have an alias for the cluster's IP address on the loopback interface. Then, the server sends a response back to the client by inverting the source and destination IP addresses from the original packet received. This way, the server can respond directly to the client.

The fact that the server can respond directly to the client makes it possible to have a small bandwidth network for incoming traffic, such as Ethernet or token-ring, and a large bandwidth network for outgoing traffic, such as Asynchronous Transfer Mode (ATM) or Fiber Distributed Data Interface (FDDI).

2.1.2 High availability

The Dispatcher has a high availability feature. It involves the use of a secondary machine that monitors the main, or primary, machine and stands by to take over the task of load balancing, should the primary machine fail at any time.

In case of failure, clients lose only the current connections, but they can immediately establish a new connection to the remaining servers with no problems. The high-availability environment involves two Dispatcher machines with connectivity to the same clients, and to the same cluster of servers, as well as connectivity between the Dispatchers. Both of the Dispatchers must be using the same operating systems.

The two Dispatcher machines are usually referred to as *primary* machine and *backup* machine:

- The primary machine works normally as a Dispatcher, and is in the *active* state while it is balancing the load among the servers of its clusters.

- The backup machine, configured in a very similar way to the primary machine, stays in *standby* mode unless the primary fails.

The two machines are synchronized, and only the primary machine routes packets, while the backup machine is continually updated.

The two machines establish communication to monitor the status of each other, referred to as a *heartbeat*, using a port that you can choose. If the primary machine fails, the backup machine detects this failure, switches to active state, and begins to take over the routing of packets. When the primary machine is operational again, but in standby state, you can either decide that it again *automatically* becomes the active machine, or leave it in standby mode. In this case, you will have to activate it *manually* if you want it to booome the active machine again. See Figure 4.

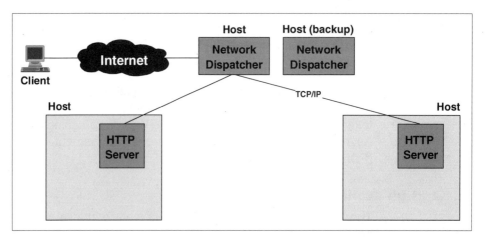

Figure 4. IBM Network Dispatcher

2.2 Servlet load balancing

IBM WebSphere Advanced Edition installation comprises one or more Web server plug-ins.

The plug-ins allow Application Server to extend Web server capabilities. Combined with Application Server and its Web server plug-in, a Web server can handle requests for servlets, enterprise beans, and other Java components. The plug-in configuration specifies how the Web server using it can recognize valid requests for resources managed by the Application Server product. This configuration is dynamic, meaning you do not have to stop the Web servers and start them again to cause the Web servers to recognize configuration changes made in the WebSphere Administrative Console.

As we will create servlet engines whose clones will reside on a machine other than the machine containing the Web server, we need to create and enable servlet redirectors. Servlet redirectors reside on the same machine as the Web server, using Inter-ORB Protocol (IIOP) to route servlet requests to clones on remote machines, behind the inner firewall.

You will see that the redirector allows you to separate your Web server from your administrative servers, application servers, and databases, which makes sense when setting up a DMZ configuration.

When the Web server receives HTTP requests, it uses the OSE transport to route requests to servlet engines having only local clones. The OSE transport utilizes push-based native load balancing.

When the Web server receives HTTP requests to servlet engines having both local and remote, it uses an OSE transport to pass the requests to the servlet redirector. Note that the servlet redirector handles the requests for both clones, even though one of the clones is local to the Web server. The servlet redirector uses Internet Inter-ORB Protocol (IIOP) to route requests to the local and remote clones.

IIOP is more flexible than OSE, allowing remote distribution of clones, with a 15-30% slight performance degradation. Like OSE, IIOP performs load balancing.

When the Web server receives HTTP requests to servlet engines having only remote clones, it again uses the servlet redirector to route the requests off the local machine.

You have three ways of setting up a servlet redirector:

- Thin (XML-based) servlet redirector
- Thick servlet redirector with full administration server
- Thick servlet redirector with administration agent

The thin servlet redirector is a standalone process based on the XML configuration. It does not run as part of the administrative server, meaning it does not require database access. The drawback of this configuration is that it does not support the IBM WebSphere Advanced Edition security features (authentication/authorization). Besides, it cannot be managed through the graphical administrative console.

The thick redirector runs as part of the IBM WebSphere Advanced Edition administrative server. You can configure and manage it through the administrative console. The drawbacks of this configuration are that it requires the overhead of running a fully-fledged administrative server, including access to the database repository through the inner firewall.

The last configuration is the one we chose. Here the administrative server runs in "agent" mode: it attaches to another administrative server process, running behind the firewall, and uses that admin server to connect to the WAS repository. This way we get the best of both worlds: we minimize the number of processes running on the Web server machine (no DB2 nor DB2 client required), and still enable security.

The servlet redirector (Figure 5) is an instance of `com.ibm.servlet.engine.ejs.IIOPRedirector` that uses an instance of `com.ibm.servlet.engine.ejs.RemoteSRPBean` as a target for dispatching URLs.

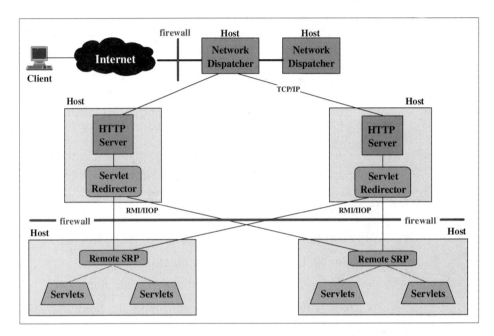

Figure 5. Servlet redirector

The servlet redirector directs the requests for URLs to the servlet engine clones based on a given server selection policy. This policy defines how clients choose among server clones (instances) within a server group.

The possible values are:

- **Random**: Server instances are selected randomly from a server group.

- **Round robin**: A server instance is initially selected at random from an ordered list. Other server instances are selected from the ordered list in turn, until the initially selected server is selected again. If a particular server instance is stopped or otherwise unavailable, that instance is skipped (no attempt is made to select it) until the next iteration through the server list.

For each policy you can also specify whether you want to make local (in-process) calls if possible. This is what is called *preferlocal*.

Remote OSE

Another possibility that became available with IBM WebSphere Advanced Edition 3.02 Fixpack 1 ("3.021") is to use Remote OSE. Remote OSE enables the Web server to forward requests to a servlet engine on a remote machine. Remote OSE is preferred in most cases over the servlet redirector, because it is faster, easier to configure, and runs through Network Address Translation (NAT) firewall. However, it lacks secure transport.

2.2.1 Cloning

IBM WebSphere Advanced Edition supports both horizontal and vertical scaling (see Figure 6):

- Horizontal scaling consists in distributing work among many machines, some or all of which can be less powerful. Failover is a main advantage of horizontal scaling. If a machine becomes unavailable, its work can be routed to other machines containing server clones. We also use IBM SecureWay Network Dispatcher for "spraying" requests to identical multiple machines, each running an application server clone, or a servlet redirector (which one is chosen is not relevant for this part of the discussion). This does not interfere, but rather complements the workload management provided automatically by IBM WebSphere Advanced Edition cloning.

- Vertical scaling consists in using this cloning support so as to get more from each machine on which the product runs. A server and several of its clones can share the same machine, enabling you to utilize more of the machine's resources, such as CPU. This works well when the individual machines in your topology are powerful but under-utilized.

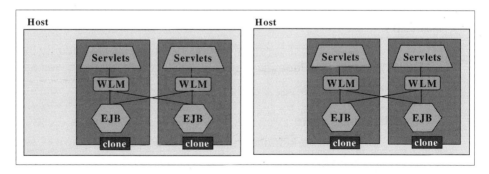

Figure 6. Clones Including Servlets and Enterprise Beans

So, when you clone your application for workload management (WLM), failover, and vertical scaling:

- Changes to a model are propagated to all of the clones associated with that model, so requests can be routed to any one of them, with the same results. Work can therefore be shared to improve throughput of client remote method invocations. This is the "load-balancing" benefit.

- With several clones available to handle requests, and distributed to various nodes, an entire machine can fail without producing devastating consequences (unless, of course, the failed machine is a single point of failure). Requests can be routed to other nodes if one node fails.

Cloning is not just for distributed environments. Another reason to clone servers and other instances is vertical scaling.

2.3 Servlets/EJB load balancing

Requests, from servlets and/or EJBs, to EJBs, can be WLMed in the same kind of way.

Basically what you do is the same: configure the application server you want to clone, deploy into it the enterprise beans that you plan to clone, create a model of the server and then use the server model for creating one or more new clones.

The only tricky part is to use the "wlmjar" command against the deployed JAR file of the enterprise bean to produce a WLM-enabled JAR file (VisualAge for Java does that by default).

By combining all the elements described above you can build a reliable and scalable configuration as depicted in Figure 3 on page 7.

2.4 Security

For such a configuration, we still need to enforce security by introducing firewalls and identification/authentication of users as well as resources access control.

2.4.1 Demilitarized zone

A DMZ network configuration has three separate network segments: the public network, the DMZ, the enterprise network.

The public network is where client requests originate.

The DMZ is where the HTTP servers are installed. Each HTTP server machine must contain a WebSphere standalone servlet redirector to give the Web server access to the protected WebSphere application servers on machines inside the enterprise network. The DMZ is protected from the public network by a firewall, which limits the traffic allowed to enter and leave the network segment.

The enterprise network is where the WebSphere administrative server, administrative repository, and application server processes are installed. It is also where the company's databases and sensitive systems typically reside. This segment is protected from the DMZ by a second firewall, which further limits the traffic allowed to enter it from the DMZ.

Databases may:

- Hold user and session data, support applications
- Keep administrative data for the application servers

They can also present a security risk by making your firewall more vulnerable. So with database accesses through the inner firewall only, the DMZ configuration helps you minimize your risk. To get into the enterprise network, an intruder would have to break through both firewalls, including the outer firewall that has no weak spots in terms of database accesses.

2.4.2 Authentication and authorization

Authentication is the process of finding that a user is really who he says he is. This is done by implementing user ID and password lookup scheme. IBM WebSphere Advanced Edition can be configured to use SecureWay Directory, which is a Lightweight Directory Access Protocol (LDAP) based directory server that provides a common and simple method for centrally storing, locating and managing directory information on an enterprise network across multiple platforms.

Authorization, on the other hand, is the process of determining if that person has rights to use a secured resource in some way, for example, the right to invoke a method on an EJB. Authorization consists of two steps: security lookup and rule enforcement.

- Security lookup – the receiver of a request uses the known identity of the caller to determine what access rights the caller possesses. Most commonly, the access rights are represented as a set of groups obtained from a file or directory.

- Rule enforcement – the receiver uses the caller's access rights and compares them against some set of rules to determine if access should be allowed or denied based on the action requested. Most commonly, the rule is represented as an Access Control List (ACL). These rules are defined in IBM WebSphere Advanced Edition.

On a future release, it may be possible to use an LDAP directory to store users access rights and manage them via policy management tools.

We have seen the different components that provide a scalable, reliable infrastructure to support the design of our e-business application in a secured environment.

In the next step, we decompose an application in a three tier model and analyze specific design considerations.

Chapter 3. Support for pervasive computing

In this section, we describe how the design for a Web browser client can be adapted to other types of clients.

3.1 Pervasive computing and its impact

The convergence of computing, telecommunications, and consumer electronics is causing a tremendous growth in the number and variety of mobile computing devices. The market spans over a multitude of emerging devices including laptops, PDAs (for example Palm Pilot, Workpad or Psion) and mobile appliances (such as mobile phones, pagers and wearable devices). Mobile enablement is a key component in an e-business application. Figure 7 shows pervasive devices in our scenario.

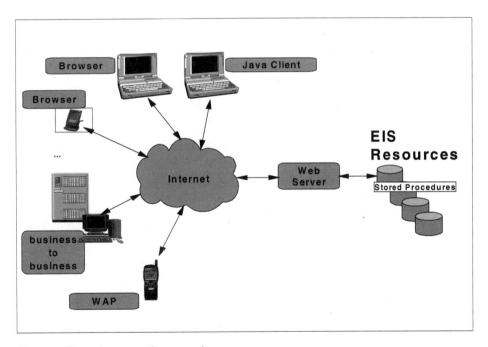

Figure 7. Pervasive computing scenario

3.2 Problems with supporting multiple types of clients

Mobile computing with its remote and bandwidth constrained connections makes application and data access more challenging.

To provide mobile users and business partners access to business data and applications, the architecture must address these challenges:

- Most mobile links are slow and unreliable
- Different device output capabilities (small screen size, gray-scale)
- Different user input capabilities (pen, voice, buttons, keyboard)
- Business to consumer vs. business to business communications
- Some devices are capable of using Java technology, and some are not

The clients differ not only in the user interface but in the functionality. In the design of our architecture, we need to pay attention to different device types with all their peculiarities.

3.3 Description of the solution

To handle multiple types of clients, the content must be adapted to the capabilities of the client device. Here are two solutions:

1. The application can provide **filters** for different output devices. A filter may reduce the amount of data by discarding data that the device is incapable of using or displaying, or is unwilling to wait for. For example, images can be discarded when the client can only display text.

2. The application can be aware of a device's capabilities. Then it is possible to **target** the information specifically for that device.

3.3.1 Provide filters for different output devices

The first solution to filter the data for the different output devices has effects on the choice of technologies used to build the view of our architecture. In case of JavaServer Pages, a solution is to have multiple JSPs, one for each output device per servlet. The servlet has to examine the output device and select the right JSP for the current device.

This approach is easy to implement, but it is limited to JavaServer Pages. Another — a better — way to satisfy the request to a pervasive friendly architecture could be the separation of the output data (content) and the way of displaying this data.

One choice method is to use the *eXtensible Markup Language (XML)*. XML is a simple, cross-platform and extensible way of structuring data. It was defined and standardized by the World Wide Web Consortium[1]. XML is a text-based tag language like HTML. In contrast to HTML, XML treats documents as data and not as formatted text. So, XML markup states what data *is*, HTML markup states how the data should be *displayed*.

To render XML documents, the W3C defined the eXtensible Stylesheet Language (XSL). With XSL it is possible to generate HTML and also PDF or TeX documents.

In business to business communication there are computers on both ends, which have to interpret the content rather than display it. XML is excellent for those kind of applications, because both sides have direct access to the data.

In summary, one solution for filtering is to first determine the client type. Then, the servlet is executed as normal but its output shows an XML-stream with a stylesheet regarding the type of client (Figure 8).

A variation of this, which is useful in many scenarios, would process the XML document and the XSL stylesheet on the server within the servlet. There are a few advantages to this approach:

- Security and also network performance: Only the necessary data get to the client, the rest is filtered on the server.

- Fewer requirements of a client: Because the conversion is done on the server (which is scalable), the client does not have to interpret the XML/XSL. This frees up the client CPU, the client memory as well as the client from interpreting XML.

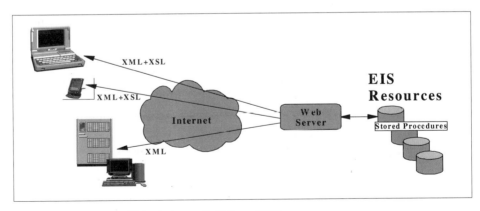

Figure 8. Satisfying multiple devices with XML and XSL

[1] see http://www.w3.org

3.3.2 Target different types of client devices

The second solution mentioned above, to target the different types of client devices, is more complicated to implement. But in complex applications it will be necessary to proceed this way. Support of multiple types of client does not only mean to provide multiple stylesheets or JavaServer Pages. Even if HTTP is typically used in e-business applications, not all devices may communicate via HTTP, there may be the need to use a pure socket communication or the RMI protocol for example. And because of the different output capabilities (small display) there may be the need for a device type to split one output page into many pages. We have to remark that these pages represent the same business logic than the one page we had before.

Because the task that has to be done is still the same, we need to name and to define this task by introducing an **activity business object**. An activity business object is a business domain motivated task which is normally run by only one person and is usually finished within one session. During a standard object oriented methodology, an activity business object can be found by the use case analysis and corresponds to an use case.

For the distinction between reusable parts of the activity business object and parts which have to be re-implemented for each type of client, we can split an activity into model, view and controller.

The model is the reusable part of an activity and can be shared for all client devices. It implements the logic of the activity without knowing anything about the presentation of the activity. The model defines services which are used by the controller. There is only one model per activity.

The responsibility of the controller is the definition of the work flow within the activity. Because this work flow depends on the client device, it is necessary to have multiple controllers, one for each device type. Since some devices implement similar or identical functionality, it may be possible to reuse some of the code. As said before the controller handles the application behavior. This includes:

- Selecting the view to display
- Interpreting client events, such as which button was pressed

Client events are strongly device dependent. A browser, for example, is able to trigger a "button-pressed" event, whereas, it is not possible to get a "focus lost" event; however, it is available by a Java client.

The view is specific to each different type of device. Many techniques may be used to implement the view for plain HTML, JSP, or XSL. The view may even be a Java applet or application which communicates with the server via RMI.

The activity business object does not know which technology is used to transfer the data to the client. That means that the controller has to be separated from the communication to the client. According to our architecture, the servlet communicates with the client, therefore we need one servlet per communication technology used. The complete architecture is shown in Figure 9.

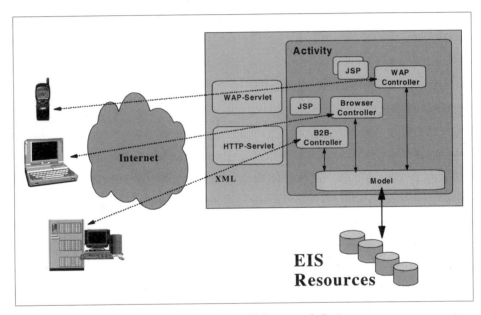

Figure 9. Architecture overview for handling multiple types of clients

Chapter 4. WebSphere command framework

In this chapter we describe the command pattern and the command framework which is the base for all commands. We capture the basic concepts of commands and provide an extendable infrastructure for their implementation. In addition, we capture the use of commands.

4.1 Command pattern

Given the structure suggested for e-business applications, the business logic of an interaction is isolated from the work flow and the view by using the Model-View-Controller paradigm. This leads us to the three components of program logic as shown in Figure 10:

- The **user interface logic** is the **view** and contains the logic which is necessary to construct the presentation.

- The **servlet** acts as the **controller** and contains the logic which is necessary to process user events and to select an appropriate response.

- The **business logic** is the **model** and accomplishes the goal of the interaction. This may be a query or an update to a database.

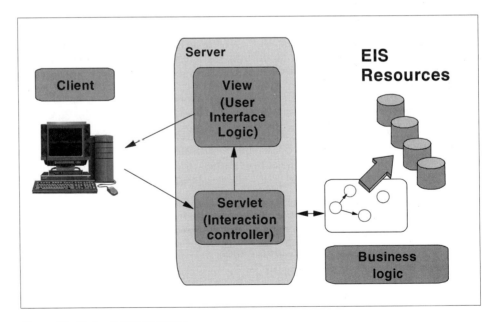

Figure 10. Web application model

It is critical to maintain a clean separation between the different types of program logic, because the link between the servlet and the business logic is especially sensitive. As the reason for that we have to face several more problems in the communication between these layers, such as:

- **Problems with performance:** The granularity of artifacts on the server (that is, objects, tables, procedure calls, and so on) often causes a single client-initiated business logic request to involve several round-trip messages between client and server, which consumes a significant amount of system resources. This may include several calls to perform the business task and several more calls to retrieve the results of that task. This can cause efficiency concerns and make programming difficult.

- **Problems with stability:** Changes in the business logic may affect the servlet if the interface of the business logic (for example, the EJB) is modified. As a consequence all servlets using that business logic must be changed.

- **Problems with implementing the technology:** There are several possible technologies for how business logic can be implemented. This includes EJB, JDBC or the Common Connector Framework. In addition to different implementation programming models, each of these technologies has a different way to invoke a request to execute business logic. That means that the servlet has to be aware of all used technologies and has to implement interfaces to them.

Additionally, we may run into problems when calling EJB directly from the servlets. This communication is being based on RMI/IIOP and has significant deployment problems when passing through a firewall.

4.1.1 Commands

A good way to solve the above problems and a good way to separate the program logic is by the use of **commands**. Commands encapsulate business logic tasks and provide a standard way to invoke the business logic request and access to data using a single round-trip message.

A command is a stylized Java class with the following characteristics:

- A command object corresponds to a specific business logic task, such as a query or an update task.

- A command has a simple, uniform usage pattern.

- A command hides the specific connector interfaces and logic from the servlet.

- A command can cache information retrieved during the business task.

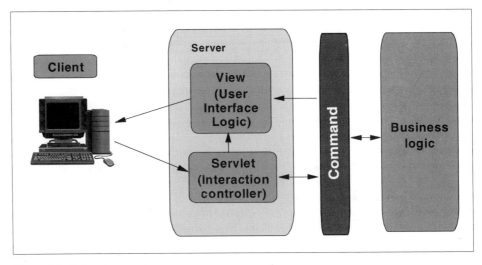

Figure 11. Using commands

Commands are used as shown in Figure 11, where the servlet instantiates a command object. Then, the servlet sets the input parameter of the command and executes it. When the command has finished performing the business logic, the result, if any, is stored in the command, so that the servlet or the view can get the result values by interrogating the command object.

We recommend that you implement the command as a JavaBean, that is, a java class with naming restrictions:

- There must be a method defined for each input property xxx:

```
void setXxx (Xxx xxx);
```

- There must be a method defined for each output property:

```
Xxx getXxx ();
```

4.1.2 Display commands

In our programming model the command bean can be interrogated by the standard bean mechanism. That means that a JSP programmer has to have knowledge about Java programming since the output properties of a command may include complex structures, such as arrays.

To solve the problem we introduce *display commands*. The idea is to eliminate any handwritten code in the JSP, therefore, supporting a development model in which non-programmers can develop, modify, and maintain presentations. Display commands are commands except that they are intended to run locally. A display command calls other commands to run the business logic and encapsulates all the dynamic content of the page by converting the output properties of the executed command into HTML.

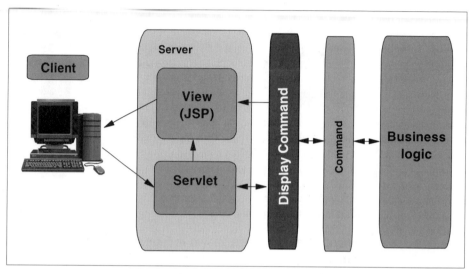

Figure 12. Using Display Commands

4.1.3 Application developer roles

The e-business applications are created by multidisciplinary teams. The skills required are contributed from graphic artists, Web page designers, client and server side script writers, and Java programmers.

Whether there is only one person or one hundred, the concept of the separation of roles and responsibilities is key to the successful creation and maintenance of the e-business application (see Figure 13).

The command pattern involves separating the tasks by each role, such as:

- The *HTML Developer* uses a tool like WebSphere Page Designer to generate HTML pages and JSP templates.

- The *Script Developer* uses a Java programming environment like VisualAge for Java to edit, test and debug servlets and JSPs.

- The *Java Business Logic Developer* uses a Java programming environment, like VisualAge for Java, and builders, like the integrated EJB Builder, to specify the details of the business logic, to access legacy applications and data, and to build the commands.

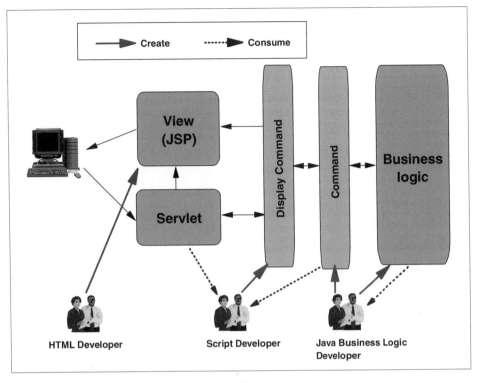

Figure 13. Separation of Roles and Responsibilities

4.1.4 The value of commands

Commands add a valued layer to the e-business architecture and they give us the following advantages:

- Because commands are implemented as serialized objects, they can be shipped to and executed within any Java environment, within any server supporting Java access to its resources and providing a protocol to copy the command between the command client JVM and its JVM. The protocol does not have to be IIOP. This gives the opportunity of enhancing the performance and the deployment (firewall) by executing the command on the enterprise server.

- Commands allow an application to be partitioned into efficient units of client-server interaction.

- Commands allow the caching of data.

- As commands are implemented as JavaBeans, it is easy to get access to the output data. Therefore, it is possible to store an executed command bean in a session environment of a servlet and use it by a JSP.

- Commands can even be used or integrated in most Web design tools like IBM WebSphere Studio, because they are implemented as JavaBeans.

- The servlet code is independent of the style of the command's implementation and it is independent of where the command is physically executed.

- Another advantage of choosing the command pattern approach is that it facilitates a cleaner separation of roles in a development team.

- The use of commands leads to a stable boundary between business logic and user-interface logic.

4.1.5 Command granularity

The command pattern can be used to reduce the overhead of cross-tier communication.

There is no perfect answer to the trade-off between good interface design and a reduced communication overhead. Our proposal is, that the requesting tier (the servlet) of a communication has to design the commands exactly to support its tasks. The idea is, that a servlet should only execute one command per invocation which encapsulates all of the controller function except for the HTTP request parsing. That means when implementing an e-business application, the servlet only interprets the HTTP request and executes commands. As a consequence of this approach we will get as many commands as we have server interactions for a given use case.

4.1.6 Relationship of command beans and EJB session beans

An obvious question is: Why not use IIOP to session beans to accomplish the same objective as commands? The answer is that commands have the following advantages:

- Command beans handle multiple protocols to accommodate any target server, not just IIOP to EJB servers. This includes, of course, IIOP but also HTTP.

- When acting in a distributed environment, command beans require fewer round-trip messages. For a session bean EJB whose container runs in a separate server, several remote messages are required to do a single logical request:

    1. Look up the home

2. Narrow the home

3. Create the session bean instance

4. Call the method

5. Destroy the session bean instance

Steps 1 and 2 can often be cached, but there are still three round-trip messages required per instance.

4.1.7 Caching

Using commands, the cross-tier communication is reduced to one round-trip per task. Caching is a technology which can be used to reduce this to even less than one.

Caching is not a new technique; it is a general principle that can be used to reduce cross-tier communication, database queries and computation.

The principle of caching is simple: Don't ask a question twice if you can do it once and save the result to use the second time. This principle can be difficult to implement since the amount of saved data may become unmanageable and the results can be reused only if they are still accurate.

In e-business applications, there are two types of information that can be cached:

- Formatted information such as whole or partial HTML pages can be cached. This works well when many people need to view the same material presented in the same way, such as on a sports or news site. Caching partial pages adds the flexibility to customize pages for users while still retaining many of the benefits of caching. Since View Commands represent partial HTML pages it makes sense to cache those commands.

- Data can be cached. This works well when the same data needs to be viewed in different ways. This means that commands (for example, which are executed by the view commands) can be cached.

The two types can be used together. For example, a commerce site may cache product descriptions in a formatted form while caching customer-profile information as data.

4.2 Pattern description

The complete command hierarchy is shown in Figure 14, with the `command` interface as the base for all commands. Each command has to implement at least the `Command` interface. The set of methods defined in the `Command` interface are — besides the creation and initialization of the command — the only methods that a client of the command has to know about.

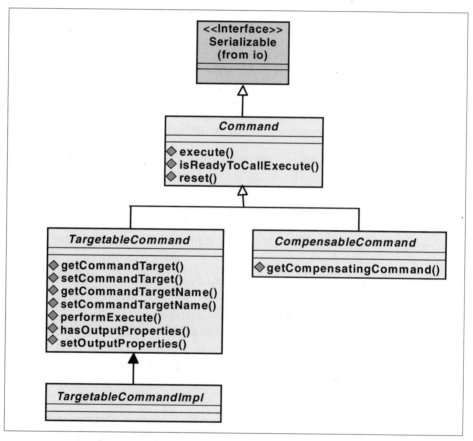

Figure 14. Command structure

For each specific command class, some input properties are required and others are optional. A client can test whether all required input properties have been set by calling:

```
public boolean isReadyToCallPerform ();
```

A client actually executes a command by calling:

```
public void execute () throws CommandException;
```

It is sometimes convenient to reuse the same command instance. For example, there may be several complex input parameters and only one of them needs to change for the next execution. This is enabled by calling:

```
public void reset ();
```

This resets the output properties to the values they had prior to the execute method being called.

4.2.1 Command states

A command bean can enter three states. After creation the bean resides in the *new* state if properties have to be set. After the last required property has been set, the command steps to the *initialized* state. In this state, and only in this state, the method `isReadyToCallPerform()` should return `true` and the `execute()` method may be called. This method moves the command from the *initialized* state to the *executed* state as illustrated in Figure 15. The command may be moved into the *initialized* state again by calling the `reset()` method.

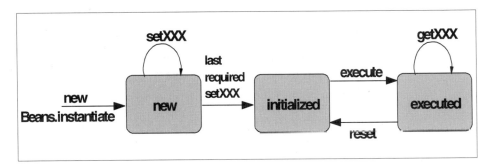

Figure 15. State diagram of a command bean

4.2.2 Command target

To distribute a command bean, more complexity is involved. The command framework introduces a command target to deal with this complexity (see Figure 16).

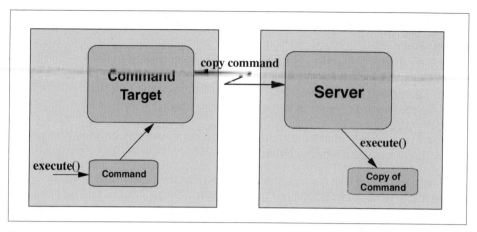

Figure 16. Remote execution of a command

A command target is responsible for the proper execution of a command in a target server environment. In a distributed environment, this may involve the following steps:

- Copying the command over a server-specific protocol (for example, RMI) to the target server's JVM

- Executing the command in the target server's JVM

- Copying the executed command back to the client's JVM

For each target server environment, there can be one or more classes that implement the CommandTarget interface.

The CommandTarget interface is a wrapper interface for a target server JVM where a command can be executed. As seen in Figure 17, because it extends the java.rmi.Remote interface, it can potentially be an Enterprise JavaBean.

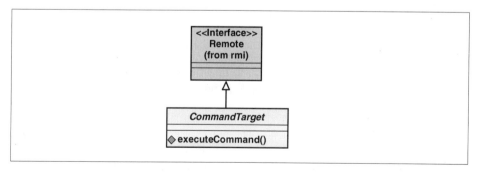

Figure 17. CommandTarget model

The only method defined in this interface is:

```
public TargetableCommand executeCommand (TargetableCommand)
```

This is called by the `execute()` method of a targetable command.

4.2.3 Targetable command

The command framework defines a *targetable command* as a command which can be executed in a command target environment. A targetable command includes an interface and an implementation of the logic to distribute a command.

The `TargetableCommand` interface is an extension of the `Command` that allows a command to be redirected to a particular `CommandTarget` for execution. This is done by the abstract class `TargetableCommandImpl` which implements the `execute()` method of the command.

The implementation is called by the command client and handles the distributed issues. Because of this, a different method is needed for the implementation of the business logic, which is defined in the `TargetableCommand` and which is called by the implementation of the command target:

```
public void performeExecute ();
```

There are two ways for a command client to specify which execution environment (command target) is used for a command prior to calling the `execute()` method:

- The CommandTarget can be set by the command client directly via the following method:
  ```
  public void setCommandTarget (CommandTarget commandTarget);
  ```
- The CommandTarget bean name can be set by the command client via the following method:
  ```
  public void setCommandTargetName (String targetName);
  ```

An additional aspect handled by the TargetableCommand is a performance improvement. The method is defined in the TargetableCommand interface:

```
public boolean hasOutputProperties ()
```

It is implemented in the `TargetableDefaultImpl`. It returns the value of the `hasOutputProperties` instance variable. That variable should be set by the command implementation. A false shows that the command does not have output properties. That can eliminate unnecessary copying and message overhead.

The TargetableCommand defines a method, which is used to copy all output properties from a given command to another command (of the same type):

```
public void setOutputProperties (TargetableCommand fromCommand);
```

This operation is necessary because the executed command will be shipped back to the client side where the output properties have to be copied back to the original command. The TargetableCommandImpl provides a default implementation where introspection is used to copy all instance variables, provided that all instance variables are non-private and non-package.

4.2.4 Compensable command

In some cases it may be useful to have an *undo* function for a command. Although the undo function may be provided as a base function of a command pattern, there are many cases in which a command cannot be undone. Therefore, it is appropriate to have two commands. For example, a MakeReservation command may have a CancelReservation command as a reverse command.

The command framework offers the ability to associate two commands in a way that one compensates the other (for example, does the best possible job of reversing its action). The compensable command represents the "undo" command. Therefore, a CompensableCommand interface which extends the Command interface is defined by the framework (see Figure 18).

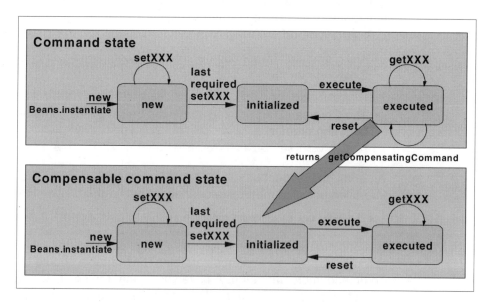

Figure 18. Command and Compensable command state diagram

The `CompensableCommand` interface introduces one method, which returns the initialized compensable command ready to be executed:

```
public Command getCompensatingCommand ();
```

That means that the input properties of the compensable commands are already set. The state of the command itself does not change.

4.2.5 Target policy

To determine which CommandTarget is used for which TargetableCommand, a policy has to be established. Therefore the command framework provides the `TargetPolicy` interface to allow different policies to be plugged into the framework. The interface shown in Figure 19 has one method:

```
public CommandTarget getCommandTarget (TargetableCommand command);
```

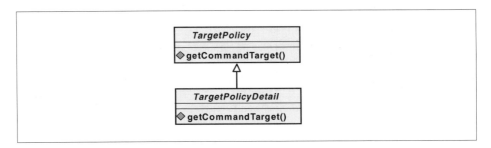

Figure 19. TargetPolicy interface

The framework provides a default implementation in the `TargetPolicyDefault` class adding the following methods to register and unregister a mapping between a targetable command and a command target:

```
public void registerCommand (String commandBeanName,
                             String targetBeanName);
public void unregisterCommand (String commnadBeanName);
```

The default policy contains the following:

1. If the TargetableCommand contains a CommandTarget (obtained via the `TargetableCommand.getCommandTarget()` method), use it.

2. Otherwise, if the TargetableCommand contains a CommandTarget bean name (obtained via the `TargetableCommand.getCommandTargetName()` method), use it.

3. Otherwise, if the TargetPolicyDefault contains a registered mapping between a command bean and a CommandTarget name (set via the `TargetPolicyDefault.registerCommand()` method), use it.

4. Otherwise, if a default target bean name has been set (set via the `TargetPolicyDefault.setDefaultTargetName()` method), use it.

5. Otherwise, return null.

4.2.6 Interaction between the objects

To see how the command framework works, Figure 20 shows the integration between the objects involved in executing a TargetableCommand.

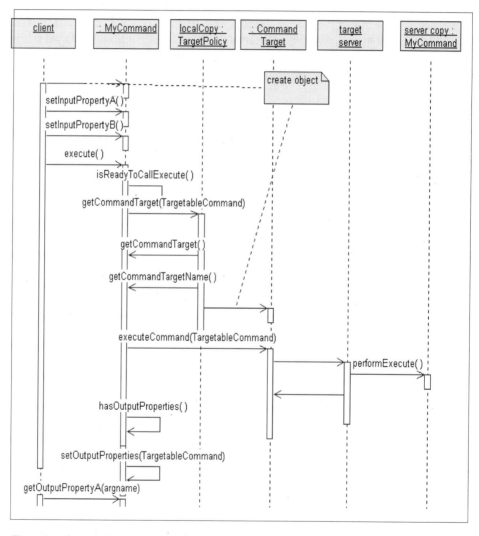

Figure 20. Sequence diagram of a command

The client has to create a command bean to set the required input properties and call its execute() method. This method, implemented by the TargetableCommandImpl class, first checks if it is in the *initialized* state.

Then, the command asks the target policy for a command target. If the default target policy is used, it uses the strategy described above. The policy creates a new command target; and the command calls the command target for execution by using the executeCommand() method. Since we are executing a targetable command, the command target copies the command to the server where its performExecute() method is called. If the command has output properties (which is determined by calling its hasOutputProperties() method), it is replicated back to the client side, where the original command copies its output properties from the replicated command with the setOutputProperties() method. Finally, the command client can access the output properties of the command.

4.2.7 Command exceptions

The command framework defines several exceptions (Figure 21).

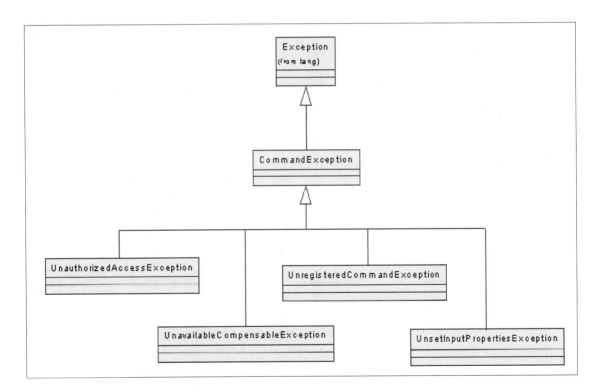

Figure 21. Command exceptions

All exceptions defined by the framework derive from CommandException:

- An UnsetInputPropertiesException is thrown, when a client calls the execute() method while not all required input properties have been set.

- The TargetableCommandImpl throws an UnregisteredCommandException, if the TargetPolicy null, which means that no command target could be found.

- When a CompensableCommand has no compensating command to return, it has to throw an UnavailbleCompensableCommandException.

- A command may implement authorization. The command can throw an UnauthorizedAccessException when the client attempts to execute a command without access authorization.

4.3 Command programming model

Before implementing a command the command programmer has to decide whether the command will be executed only locally or if it may be executed on a remote server. Command beans that execute locally (that is, in the same JVM as the calling servlet) simply implement the Command interface. If a command is to execute remotely on another server, it implements TargetableCommand by extending the TargetableCommandImpl class.

If you want to provide an undo command which is associated to the command, you have to implement the CompensableCommand interface within the first command.

To show an example we implement a targetable command used in the Patterns Development Kit. Check the Web site:

http://www-4.ibm.com/software/developer/web/patterns/

It is called SaveReadingsCommand and stores a hashtable in a DB2 database. It extends the abstract base class TargetableCommandImpl:

```
public class SaveReadingsCommand extends TargetableCommandImpl implements
Serializable
{}
```

A command may require some input properties. Because the command class should be a JavaBean, it is recommended that the command follows the standard JavaBean naming guidelines. That means that the input parameter is JavaBean input properties and should have a signature:

```
public void setXX (XXX xxx)
```

The output parameter should be JavaBean output properties with a signature:

```
public YYY getYYY ()
```

In our example, we want the command client to set the user ID and the password for accessing a database. In addition, we want the client to input a hashtable with the weather readings that are going to be stored in the database. We get the following attribute definition:

```
private Hashtable readings = null; // Hashtable to hold readings
 private String userId = null; // Instance variable for Database Userid
private String password = null; // Instance variable for Database password
```

And, the set-methods for these are:

```
public void setPassword(String password) {
    this.password = password;
}
public void setReadings(Hashtable readings) {
    this.readings = readings;
}
public void setUserId(String userId) {
    this.userId = userId;
}
```

To check, whether all required properties have been set, we have to implement the method `public boolean isReadyToCallPerform ()`. In our example we get:

```
public boolean isReadyToCallExecute() {
    return true;
}
```

Finally, since we are developing a distributed command, we have to implement the `performExecute()` method with the business logic.

Sometimes it is not desired that the client of a command has full access to the command bean class, which includes the implementation of the bean logic. Therefore, it is required to have a client part of the command and a server part. This is done by subclassing as shown in Figure 22. The command bean is used as before. Only the server knows about the server class and deserializes the server command bean instead of the client command bean.

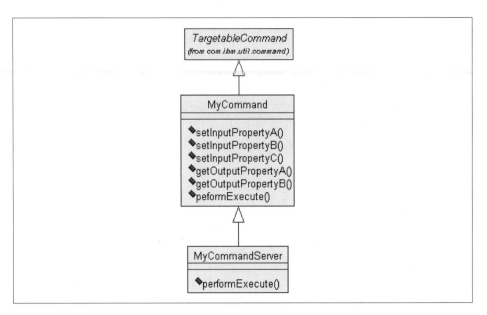

Figure 22. Splitting a Command in Client and Server

4.4 Command target and server implementation

An easy way to provide a target for executing commands in the same Java environment is the use of a local implementation. This is done by a local command manager which is just a Java class implementing the `CommandTarget` interface. The `executeCommand()` method calls the `performExecute()` method of the command bean.

A preferred strategy using Enterprise JavaBean technology is by executing the command bean within an EJB command server.

WebSphere provides an implementation of an EJB command server as an example using a **stateless entity bean** as a command server. We define a stateless entity bean as an entity bean conforming to the EJB specification, but without having any persistent attributes. Even the primary key is not persistent. Therefore, the remote interface is defined as:

```
public interface CommandServerEntity extends CommandTarget,
javax.ejb.EJBObject {
    public TargetableCommand executeCommand(TargetableCommand command)
    throws RemoteException, CommandException;
}
```

The primary key class is provided by the code:

```
public class CommandServerEntityPrimaryKey implements java.io.Serializable
{
    public int dummy;
    final static long serialVersionUID = 3206093459760846163L;

    public boolean equals(java.lang.Object o) {
        if (! (o instanceof CommandServerEntityPrimaryKey)) {
            return false;
        }
        else
            return true;
    }

    public int hashCode() {
        return "CommandServerEntityPrimaryKey".hashCode();
    }
}
```

The CommandServerEntity can be coded as:

```
public class CommandServerEntityBean implements EntityBean {

final static long serialVersionUID = 3206093459760846163L;
private javax.ejb.EntityContext entityContext = null;
public int dummy = 0;
// All EJB specific methods must be defined
...

public TargetableCommand executeCommand(TargetableCommand command) throws
CommandException, RemoteException {
    try {
        command.performExecute();
    } catch (CommandException e) {
        /*
         * The WebSphere Advanced (3.02) Container
         * actually follows the EJB 1.1 rules for
         * exception handling.  If your business logic
         * throws a CommandException and wants to cause
         * the transaction to rollback, it must call
         * setRollbackOnly() on the bean's EJB context
         * before throwing the exception.
         *
         * Make sure that the Command Bean is using a
         * DataSource.
         */
        entityContext.setRollbackOnly();
```

```
            e.printStackTrace();
            throw e;
        } catch (Exception e) {
            e.printStackTrace(); // for trace
            if (e instanceof RemoteException) {
                RemoteException remoteException = (RemoteException)e;

                if (remoteException.detail != null) {
                 throw new CommandException(remoteException.detail);
                }
            }
            throw new CommandException(e);
        }
        if ( command.hasOutputProperties()) {
        return command;
        }
        return null;
    }

}
```

An entity bean is used instead of a session bean, so that many different transactions can access the same instance. This instance has the only distributed object stub required in the Web application. This instance can be fetched once at server startup and subsequently cached inside the EJBCommandTarget. This allows to execute a command with only one single round-trip message.

4.5 Command client model

Using a command is quite easy, as shown in Figure 23. Regardless of whether the command bean is executed locally or remotely, the client servlet executes the command bean in the same way.

First the client programmer has to instantiate the command bean he wants to use. There are several ways to instantiate a command:

- The fastest way is by use of the new-method

```
MyCommand myCommand = new MyCommand ();
```

- The standard way of instantiating a JavaBean use is:

```
MyCommand myCommand = Beans.instantiate(null,beanName);
```

Where, beanName is either a class or an instance name.

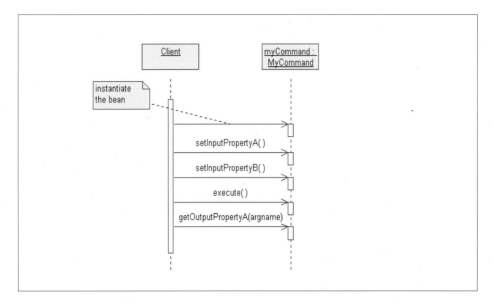

Figure 23. Using a command bean

In order to execute the command the client has to fill the input properties by calling the set-methods:

```
myCommand.setInputPropertyA ();
```

To actually invoke the business logic implemented in the command bean, the client has to call the command's `execute()`-Method:

```
myCommand.execute()
```

The command bean interacts with the back end system and stores the result as output properties. The client can access these properties with `get`-Methods:

```
a = myCommand.getOutputPropertyA ();
```

Because commands are JavaBeans, it is easy to build a simple cache for read-only commands in which the content does not change over a session time. We can store a hashtable which contains the executed command beans in the session context:

```
HttpSession session = req.getSession(false);
if (session != null) {
    Hashtable commandCache = (Hashtable) session.getValue("commandCache");
    GetPlanetListCommand menuCmd = (GetPlanetListCommand) commandCache.get
    ("topologytwo.GetPlanetListCommand");
    if (menuCmd == null) {
```

```
        // create and execute the command
        ...
        commandCache.set ("topologytwo.GetPlanetListCommand", menuCmd);
    }
    // use command results
    ...
}
```

Chapter 5. The need for EJB technology

A lot of Web sites are up and running using Java without any EJB technology. Developers have been using straight RMI objects, and managing transactions themselves using commit, rollback functionality that is built-in to JDBC without the help of application servers.

These middle tiers consist of a Java runtime and in-house developed Java classes. Some of those developers are wondering what exactly does EJB add to what they have been successfully using so far.

They got the message that EJB application servers provide container managed transactions, but typing commit() and rollback() is not that time consuming.

As with most other technologies, enterprise beans do not provide the unique solution to all your problems. But if you read the literature (prior to the availability of enterprise beans application servers) developers had to develop proprietary or buy frameworks to manage concurrency, persistence and transaction. These problems are solved, for the business logic developer, by using enterprise beans.

Once again not every application environment may benefit from using enterprise beans. To help you decide whether this technology is appropriate, this section provides some reasons to consider using it.

5.1 Multiple client types accessing shared data

Often, a single application will have multiple client types that need access to the same set of information. For instance an application may have a Web-based HTML front end for external customers, and a more complete Java application front end for internal users. Traditionally, this problem has been solved by writing two versions of the same application that share the same data sources (database tables). However, this is not efficient either in programming time or utilizating the database, if multiple database locks could be held at one time.

The EJB solution to this problem is to put common data and business logic in a single set of EJBs that are accessed by different client types (for example, Servlet/HTML and application). EJBs control access to the back-end data and internally manage the current transactions and database locking. This reduces the total programming effort by removing duplicated code in the application and by reducing the amount of effort spent in writing database control logic.

5.2 Concurrent read and update access to shared data

Traditionally, "fat client" solutions require the application to manage access to shared data at the database level. This often results in highly complex schemes to deal with database locking and concurrency, or alternatively, with the loss of data integrity when these issues are not considered.

Enterprise beans automatically handle these complex threading and simultaneous shared-data issues. As mentioned previously, enterprise beans control access to back-end data and manage the current transactions and database locking internally.

5.3 Accessing multiple datasources with transactional capabilities

Many applications require the ability to access multiple datasources. For instance, a program may use data in both a middle-tier Oracle database and a mainframe CICS or IMS system accessible through MQSeries. The key is that some applications require that this access is fully transactional – that data integrity is maintained across the datasources. For example, an application may demand that placing a user order will consist of storing the detailed order information in an Oracle database and simultaneously placing a shipment order with a CICS system through MQSeries. If either the database update or the MQ enqueuing fails, then the entire transaction should roll back.

In the past, the only choices with which to build systems like these were transaction monitors like Encina, CICS or Tuxedo, which used non-standard interfaces and required development in languages like COBOL, C or C++. Enterprise beans support multiple concurrent transactions with full commit and rollback capabilities across multiple DB2 data sources in a full 2-phase commit-capable environment.

5.4 Method-level object security

Certain types of applications have security restrictions that have previously made them difficult to implement in Java. For instance, certain insurance applications must restrict access to patient data in order to meet regulatory guidelines. Until the advent of enterprise beans there was no way to restrict access to an object or method by a particular user. Previously, restricting access at the database level, and then "catching" errors thrown at the JDBC level, or by restricting access at the application level by custom security code would have been the only implementation options.

However, enterprise beans now allow method-level security on any enterprise bean or method. Users and user groups can be created which can be granted or denied execution rights to any EJB or method. In WebSphere, these same user groups can be granted or denied access to Web resources (Servlets, JSPs and HTML pages), and the user IDs can be seamlessly passed from the Web resources to the EJBs by the underlying security framework.

5.5 Portable component-based architecture

For many of our more forward-looking customers, the key issue is that they need to achieve independence from platform, vendor, and application-server implementation. The EJB architecture, which is an industry standard component architecture, can help achieve these goals. Enterprise beans developed for WebSphere can usually be deployed on our competitor's application servers, and vice versa. This promise has been demonstrated at the June 1999 JavaOne conference where the same car dealer application was deployed on multiple enterprise bean application servers vendors. While in the short-term it is often easier and faster to take advantage of features that may precede standardization, standardization provides the best long-term advantage.

Also, customers must consider the increasing availability of tools and optimized implementations of the EJB standard that you would not get with "home grown" managed object frameworks. Since most customers are not in the middleware business, their effort can be more effectively targeted at activities that are more directly related to their business.

5.6 Multiple servers to handle throughput and availability

Over the past several years customers have found that fat-client systems simply do not scale to the thousands, or millions of users that Web-based systems may have. At the same time, software distribution problems have led to a desire to "trim down" fat clients. The 24-hour, seven-day-a-week nature of the Web has also made uptime a crucial issue for businesses. However, not everyone needs a system designed for 24x7 operation or that is able to handle millions of concurrent users. We should be able to design a system so that scalability can be achieved without sacrificing ease of development, or standardization.

So, what customers need is a way to write business logic that can scale to meet these kinds of requirements. WebSphere's EJB support can provide this kind of highly scalable, highly available system. It does this by utilizing the following features:

- Object caching and pooling: IBM WebSphere Advanced Edition automatically pools enterprise beans at the server level, reducing the amount of time spent in object creation and garbage collection. This results in more processing cycles being available to do real work.

- Workload optimization at server: IBM WebSphere Advanced Edition features EJB server cluster management. In IBM WebSphere Advanced Edition you can create server groups that span nodes. In addition, you can create "models" (abstract representations of a server) which are then "cloned" into multiple JVMs (see Figure 3 on page 7). Customers can configure clones to run on any of the server machines in the cluster. In addition, multiple clones of a single server can run on a single machine, taking advantage of multiprocessor architectures. Likewise, they can administer an entire set of "clones" as a single group. This improves availability and prevents a single point of failure in the application server.

- Cloning supports automatic failover. With several clones available to handle requests, it is more likely that failures will not damage throughput and reliability. With clones distributed to various nodes, an entire machine can fail without producing devastating consequences. All of these features happen without specifically being programmed into the system. No changes to the server-side code are necessary to take advantage of this kind of scalability.

Note that IBM WebSphere Advanced Edition supports distribution, cloning and automatic failover of other server-side Java technologies like Java Servlets and JSPs. However, these are more presentation-oriented technologies and serve as a complement to EJBs rather than as a competitor to EJBs. When uptime and scalability are key, EJBs should be a part of the overall solution.

5.7 Adopting enterprise bean technology

If you are now convinced that enterprise beans can help you in developing your applications, there is additional information that you may consider. Even though relationships are important in object-oriented programming, they are almost absent from the Enterprise JavaBeans specification.

Fortunately, IBM provides support for enterprise beans relationships with its VisualAge for Java development tool in combination with the IBM WebSphere Advanced Edition application server.

Before using this advanced feature, you need to understand the capabilities offered as well as the limitations. This is explained in Chapter 7, "Associations" on page 61.

Another important aspect of using enterprise beans is related to the way you handle collections of objects. Collections are created by way of finders but you need to figure out what's happening when invoking such finders. You may be running in two different modes: greedy or lazy. Collections and their associated modes are explained in Chapter 8, "Collections" on page 101.

With VisualAge for Java you can also improve the performance when using enterprise beans and simplify the client side code by using access beans. Access beans are generated, by VisualAge for Java, out of enterprise beans. As shown in Figure 2 on page 4, we recommend access beans as intermediaries between facade and entity beans. All this is explained in the next chapter, Chapter 6, "Access beans" on page 51.

Chapter 6. Access beans

Working with distributed objects across the network, individually calling the accessors of an enterprise bean's field, is inefficient. For that purpose, IBM has introduced access beans.

Access beans are Java components that adhere to the Sun Microsystems JavaBeans Specification and are meant to simplify the development of EJB clients. An access bean adapts an enterprise bean to the JavaBeans programming model by hiding the home and remote interfaces from the access bean user (that is, an EJB client developer). They provide fast access to enterprise beans by letting you maintain a local cache of enterprise bean attributes. Access beans make it possible to use an enterprise bean in much the same way that you would use a JavaBean.

To assist you in creating or editing access beans, VisualAge for Java provides a SmartGuide. The SmartGuide automatically saves your property settings in the repository, so that when you later generate access beans, you do not need to specify the settings again. Access beans simplify development of the Java client for enterprise beans. As shown in Figure 24, all you need to do is to invoke the constructor, set the initial arguments required for the create/find methods associated with the operation you want to perform, and invoke the remote/business methods.

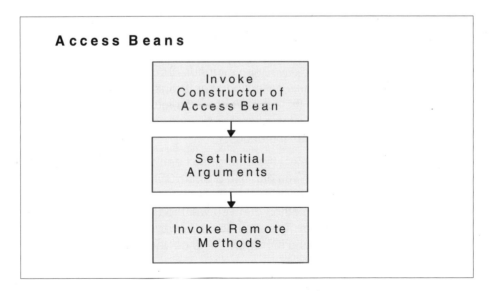

Figure 24. Access beans

Figure 25 shows access bean characteristics.

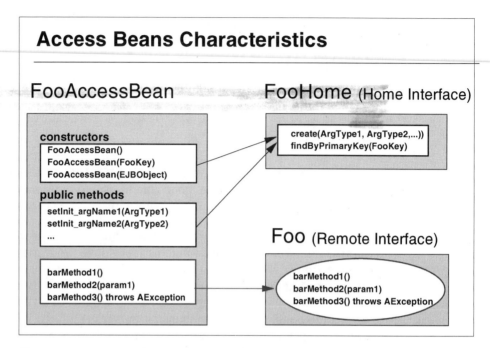

Figure 25. Access Bean Characteristics

Here we describe the general characteristics of access beans:

- Home interface methods that return a single instance of EJBObject are mapped to JavaBean constructors, while remote interface methods are mapped to JavaBean methods. Each finder method in the home interface that returns a collection of enterprise bean instances is mapped to a finder method in the access bean. You must first instantiate the access bean and then invoke the appropriate finder method that will return a collection of access bean instances.

- You can select the enterprise bean for which you want to create an access bean, then you can use a SmartGuide to customize and create the access bean. For example, the SmartGuide allows you to choose the home interface method that you want to use to map to the no-arg access bean constructor. The arguments, however, must be set by special setter methods and stored as instance variables in the access bean.

- To instantiate an enterprise bean, the access bean invokes a create() or finder method defined in the enterprise bean home interface. If a no-arg constructor is used, the access bean only instantiates the actual enterprise bean when the first business method is called.

- Access beans employ copy helper objects that are basically caches of user-selected entity bean attributes that are stored inside the access bean. The getter and setter methods for these attributes deal directly with the local cache rather than calling straight through to the remote getter and setter call. Methods are provided to flush the cache to the actual enterprise bean database and to refresh the cache from the actual enterprise bean. This can improve performance significantly for entity enterprise beans that have a large number of attributes, where issuing one remote call to get and set a large number of attributes is faster than issuing a single remote call for each.

There are three types of access beans, which are listed in ascending order of complexity:

- Java bean wrapper (for a session or entity bean)
- Copy helper (for an entity bean)
- Rowset (for multiple entity bean instances)

6.1 Wrappers

Of the three types of access beans, a JavaBean wrapper is the simplest to create. It is designed to allow either a session or entity enterprise bean to be used like a standard JavaBean and it hides the enterprise bean home and remote interfaces from you. Each JavaBean wrapper that you create extends the com.ibm.ivj.ejb.access.AccessBean class.

A JavaBean wrapper access bean has the following characteristics:

- It contains a no-arg constructor.
- When the SmartGuide prompts you to map one of the create() or finder methods defined in the home interface to the no-arg constructor of the access bean, the access bean will subsequently contain one init_xx property for each parameter of the create() or finder method that was mapped to the no-arg constructor. To simplify a JSP program that normally handles the String type, you can choose to have your access beans expose the init_xx properties as String types. However, you can also select your own converters for the init_xx properties.
- When a key class is used in the create() and finder methods for a CMP entity bean, the key fields are used as the init_xx properties instead of the key class. A key field is normally declared as a simple type. This makes it easier for visual construction tools, such as the Visual Composition Editor, to use an access bean.

- When the no-arg constructor is used, the init_xx properties must be set first before any other calls to the access bean.

- The access bean may contain several multiple-arg constructors, each corresponding to one of the create() or finder methods defined in the enterprise bean home interface.

- The access bean will perform lazy initialization when the no-arg constructor is used. When the access bean is instantiated, it will not instantiate the enterprise bean. On a remote method call, the access bean will first instantiate the remote enterprise bean if it has not yet been instantiated.

- A default JNDI name will be generated into each access bean class. The code generator will read the deployment descriptor and pass the JNDI name to the access bean. You can change the JNDI name using the setInit_JNDIName() method. It is not expected that you will need to change the JNDI name. However, in the event that an enterprise bean is deployed into a different home, the administrator may add a prefix to the JNDI name to indicate the different home.

- To look up a home, an access bean needs to obtain a name service context, which is sometimes known as the rootContext. A rootContext can be constructed if you know the name service URL and the name service type.

- Access beans provide two APIs that allow you to define a customized rootContext:

```
setInit_NameServiceTypeName()
setInit_NameServiceURLName()
```

- However, if a JSP program is running in the WebSphere run-time environment, you do not need to use these two APIs, because the rootContext is set automatically.

- An enterprise bean remote interface method can return an enterprise bean object. When this kind of method is generated in the access bean class, the return type is changed to the corresponding access bean type. This allows your user program to deal with only the access bean type and inherit the benefits provided by the access bean.

- When multiple instances of an access bean use the same home (for example, that use the same JNDI name and rootContext), the access bean class only looks up the corresponding enterprise bean home once. Each access bean class retains some class-level cache to improve the performance when instantiating an enterprise bean.

Now we take an example of creating a JavaBean wrapper type access bean for a BankAccount Bean entity bean which has a create method in its home interface that has two arguments, accountID and accountType.

By using VisualAge for Java, select your BankAccount bean and add an access bean of type **JavaBean Wrapper**. The BankAccountAccessBean gets created. The no-arg constructor of the Access bean is mapped to the create method (specified in the SmartGuide). Two setter methods are also generated for the two arguments, setInit_accountID and setInit_AccountType. The remote methods including setBalance() are created in the JavaBean. The bean is not initialized/instantiated until the first remote method is invoked. This lazy initialization is shown in Figure 26.

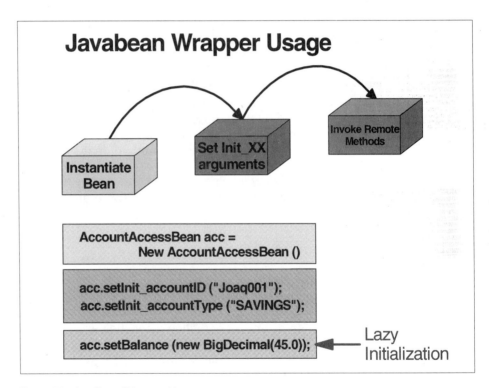

Figure 26. JavaBean Wrapper Usage

The following example shows a user program that is used to create a BankAccountAccessBean.

```
BankAccountAccessBean acc = New BankAccountAccessBean ()
acc.setInit_accountID ("Joaq001");
acc.setInit_accountType ("SAVINGS");
acc.setBalance (new BigDecimal(45.0));
```

6.2 Copy helpers

A copy helper access bean has all of the characteristics of a JavaBean wrapper, but it also incorporates a single copy helper object that contains a local copy of attributes from a remote entity bean. A user program can retrieve the entity bean attributes from the local copy helper object that resides in the access bean, which eliminates the need to access the attributes from the remote entity bean.

When you create a copy helper access bean, the remote interface of the enterprise bean will be changed to extend the CopyHelper interface as well as the EJBObject interface. You can select all of these attributes or only a subset in creating the copy helper object. The selected attributes are saved in the enterprise bean meta model. These selections are re-displayed if you decide you want to change the selection.

The copy helper object is stored inside the access bean. A get() and set() method is delegated to the local copy helper object instead of the remote enterprise bean object. To commit the changes in the copy helper to the remote enterprise bean or to refresh the local copy helper from the remote enterprise bean, your user program must call the commitCopyHelper() method and the refreshCopyHelper() method, respectively.

When you create a copy helper access bean, a copy helper interface is added to the corresponding EJBObject interface. There are two methods defined in the copy helper interface:

```
_copyToEJB()
_copyFromEJB()
```

You do not need to implement these methods. They are automatically generated into the bean class when you generate the access bean.

Now we take an example of creating a copyhelper access bean for a Bank account entity bean. By using Visual Age Java, select your BankAccount bean and add an access bean of type **Copy helper for an Entity Bean**. The BankAccountAccessBean gets created.

The following example shows a user program that is used to create a BankAccountAccessBean. In this example the code does the following:

- Create a new instance of the BankAccountAccessBean.
- Set the initial argument for the create method - init_argAccountId.
- Set the balance and accountType information.
- Commit the copy helper.

```
String accountId="Gopal001";
String balance="100.00";
String accountType="CHECKING";
try {
    itso.ejb.lab04.BankAccountAccessBean ab = new
    itso.ejb.lab04.BankAccountAccessBean();
    ab.setInit_argAccountId(accountId);
    ab.setBalance(balance);
    ab.setAccountType(accountType);
    ab.commitCopyHelper();
    System.out.println("Created Bank Account [ " + accountId + "," +
    accountType + "," +balance + "]");
} catch (Exception exc) {
System.out.println("Could not create the bank account ");
{
```

6.3 Rowsets

A rowset access bean has all of characteristics of both the Java bean wrapper and copy helper access beans. However, instead of a single copy helper object, it contains multiple copy helper objects. Each copy helper object corresponds to a single enterprise bean instance.

A rowset access bean contains a collection of copy helper objects. In turn, a copy helper object contains the primary key for each entity bean instance, but it does not contain the proxy object (the EJBObject in the EJB server) itself for the entity bean. When a session bean returns a rowset access bean as a result set, only the attributes of the entity beans are copied to the client space. The proxy objects are not copied. This is because copying a large number of enterprise bean proxy objects from the server space to the client space can cause performance problems. A JSP program can read from a rowset access bean immediately without invoking a remote call. On an update call, such as may be made using the commitCopyHelper() method, the access bean constructs the enterprise bean proxy object using the key object saved in the copy helper.

Now we take an example of creating a rowset access bean for a Bank account entity bean. By using Visual Age for Java, select your BankAccount bean and add an access bean of type **"Rowset for Multiple Entity Bean instances"**. The BankAccountAccessBean gets created.

In this example the code does the following:

- Create a new instance of the BankAccountAccessBean.
- Invoke the findAll method passing the maximum size of the result set.

- Create a new instance of the BankAccountAccessBeanTable.

- Populate the table with the access beans in the enumeration returned by the findAll method.

- Iterate through the elements in the BankAccountAccessBeanTable. For each element print the Account information in the console.

```
public static void main(java.lang.String[] args) {
try {
    BankAccountAccessBean ab = new BankAccountAccessBean();
    java.util.Enumeration en = ab.findAll(20);
    BankAccountAccessBeanTable tab = new BankAccountAccessBeanTable();
    while (en.hasMoreElements()) {
        tab.addRow((BankAccountAccessBean) en.nextElement());
    }
    for (int i=0; i < tab.numberOfRows(); i++) {
        BankAccountAccessBean ab2 = tab.getBankAccountAccessBean(i);
        System.out.println(((BankAccountKey) ab2.__getKey()).accountID +
        "," + ab2.getAccounTtype() + "," + ab2.getBalance());
    }
}catch (Exception exc) {
System.out.println("Could not retrieve BankAccounts");
}
```

6.4 Access beans and associations

If you create an access bean for an enterprise bean involved in an association. If the association has been made navigable, the navigation method returns an access bean which does not exist, and corresponding to the enterprise bean at the other side of the association.

The problem is solved by either generating the access bean corresponding to the enterprise bean at the other side of the association or if you really don't want to generate it, you need to generate the access bean first and only after the association between the enterprise beans.

6.5 Access beans and WLM

In some cases, you may need to ship access beans across the wires. This could be the case for example of a Java applet exchanging access beans with a servlet through the HTTP protocol.

The serialization of the access bean will fail because in the inheritance hierarchy of the access bean which extends AbstractEntityAccessBean and itself extends AbstractAccessBean has a private variable called myHome.

This variable is a reference to the enterprise bean home which cannot be serialized. Until VisualAge for Java Version 3.5, you needed to solve this problem by making this variable transient such that the serialization process did not attempt to save it.

6.6 Use of access beans

Now that we have seen what access beans are and brought to your attention the association and WLM problems, the question is when should we use access beans?

Access beans have been designed to improve performances when enterprise beans and their clients are separated by a network. They also provide to the client a caching mechanism for accessing homes.

In our Design Guidelines Components Environment in Figure 2 on page 4, we position access beans between the facade and entity beans. If entity beans are running in different clones, then using access beans may still improve the performances.

Access beans also could have been used between servlets and facades. Instead, we preferred to use the command framework which presents the advantage of being independent of the technology used for the business implementation. In addition, commands represent use cases that can be defined early in the development process and be used by the user interface designers. They can be easily modified and adapted to unstable requirements.

Chapter 7. Associations

VisualAge for Java 3.02 provides enhanced association support which should be deployable on any EJB 1.0 compliant EJB servers (IBM WebSphere Application Servers and others).

While some association types work with no added user code, others need EJB developer written code. Here is a synopsis of the topics discussed in this chapter:

- Section 7.1, "Overview" on page 62 identifies the tools support level for the different relation types.

- In 7.2, "Description of the association solution" on page 64 we give a detailed description of the generated code and illustrate how the inverse association maintenance works. This is a major association enhancement of VisualAge 3.02.

- In 7.3, "Association developer and user responsibilities" on page 72 we describe the required manually written code and some association usage issues, which are generated methods that do not behave as expected and should not be invoked.

- In 7.4, "Hints and tips" on page 94 we give some additional recommendations.

- Section 7.5, "Association deployment" on page 96 includes deployment considerations.

- In 7.6, "Performance impacts" on page 97 we highlight the performance aspects of the association solution and give some recommendations about how to improve the linkage performance.

The aim of this chapter is to provide supplemental information to the official VisualAge documentation (VisualAge for Java 3.02 Documentation Update, EJB Development Environment). It is not intended to provide a step-by-step introduction of the linkage usage.

7.1 Overview

The association solution supports:

- Associations between container-managed entities (CMPs)
- Associations within the same EJB Group

Bean-managed entities (BMPs) and associations across EJB Group boundaries are not supported.

7.1.1 Association types which work with no added user code

Figure 27 shows the association types which work with no added user code:

- One-to-many associations
- One-to-one associations

These have the following characteristics:

- Optional roles (0..1, 0..*) on both association ends
- Associated CMPs have independent life times, which means to delete a CMP on one end of the association does not require a cascaded delete of the bean on the other side.

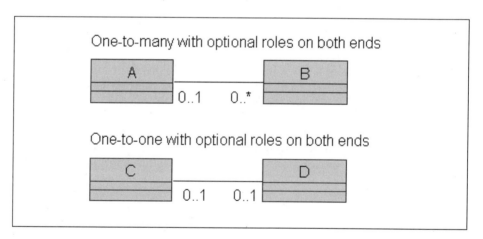

Figure 27. Association types which work with no added user code

---
   Initialization of foreign key fields ───────────────

The EJB 1.0 based container of WebSphere Advanced 3.02 does not
automatically initialize the container-managed fields in ejbCreate. This is a
EJB 1.0 spec limitation. In EJB 1.1 the container is responsible for the
proper field initialization.

For EJB 1.0 compliant containers the EJB developer has to explicitly
initialize CMP fields in ejbCreate. Because the generated foreign key fields
(see 7.2, "Description of the association solution" on page 64) are treated
as casual CMP fields, the EJB provider has to initialize the foreign key
fields in ejbCreate.

In our PersonalbankerToCustomer one-to-many sample with an optional
Personalbanker role for Customer (see Figure 30 on page 66), we have to
set the personalbanker_bankerId foreign key field to null in the ejbCreate
method of CustomerBean.

7.1.2 Association types requiring added user code or user attention

Figure 28 illustrates the association types which require added user code or
user caution when calling some generated methods:

- Many-to-many association

  A hidden table is not actively supported. In 7.3.4, "Many-to-many
  relationships" on page 88 we describe a solution with an intermediary
  CMP.

- Composition (Whole/part)

  Composition is a special aggregation type with whole/part semantics. A
  delete of a whole requires the deletion of the parts. The linkage solution
  does not support cascaded delete. In 7.3.2, "Delete cascading" on page
  77, we describe two work-arounds to achieve a delete of parts.

- Association with a required or mandatory role

  When a CMP is created with a required role the association maintenance
  has to be part of the creation. The association solution does not generate
  ejbCreate / ejbPostCreate methods. In 7.3.1, "Implementation of ejbCreate
  and ejbPostCreate methods" on page 72 we describe how to manually
  write the source.

  For some of the generated methods in an association with a required role
  occurs unexpected behavior. In 7.3.3, "Use of associations with required
  roles" on page 81, we address these critical methods.

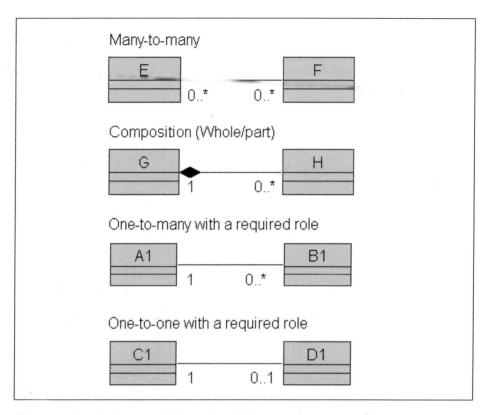

Many-to-many

Composition (Whole/part)

One-to-many with a required role

One-to-one with a required role

Figure 28. Association types which require added user code or user attention

7.2 Description of the association solution

The association solution depends on the primary, foreign key relationship. In a one-to-one association the foreign key field(s) can be held on either end, in a one-to-many relationships the EJB implementation on the single-valued end of the association holds the foreign key field(s). Members are accessed via the entity's homes.

The association solution includes runtime support and code generation at CMP creation time and at association creation and update time. The generated code is part of the development (not deployment) process.

7.2.1 Runtime support

The runtime support includes two packages:

- com.ibm.ivj.ejb.associations.links package with abstract link classes and a member enumeration (EjbMemberEnumeration) for the multi-valued association end.

- com.ibm.ivj.ejb.associations.interfaces with linkage relevant interfaces.

7.2.2 Code generation at CMP creation time

The following association specific methods are generated at CMP creation time and updated with each new or migrated association:

- _initLinks ( ), a method to initialize association links (see below) for the bean. This method is called in the ejbActivate(), ejbCreate() and ejbLoad() methods. The method invocations are generated at CMP creation time.

- _removeLinks ( ), a method to maintain the bean's associations during delete. This method is called in the ejbRemove() method. The method invocation is generated at CMP creation time.

- _getLinks ( ), a method to retrieve association links for the bean.

7.2.3 Code generation at association creation and update time

We illustrate the code generation based on the PersonalbankerToCustomer one-to-many sample (see Figure 29).

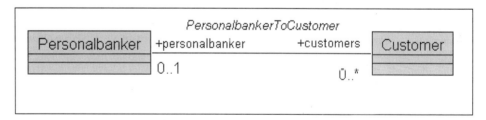

Figure 29. Personalbanker - Customer association (one-to-many)

In Figure 30 we show the Association Editor for the association.

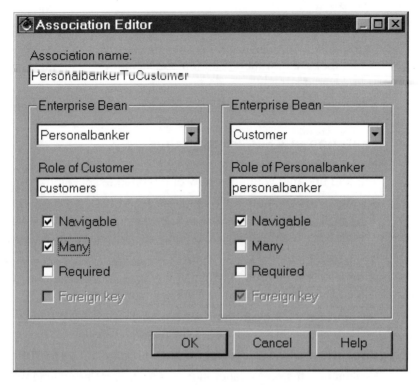

Figure 30. Association Editor for Personalbanker - Customer relationship

The following source is generated when the EJB developer clicks the **OK** button in the Association Editor:

- A concrete link class for each association end. The generated link classes are derived from one of the base classes of the runtime support, dependent on the association type.

  In our example a CustomerToPersonalbankerLink class is generated for the single-valued end of the association (Customer) and a PersonalbankerToCustomersLink class for the multi-valued end of the relationship (Personalbanker).

  Link classes insulate the CMPs from the association complexity. The Entity Beans delegate the relationship maintenance and members retrieval to the link classes.

  During runtime the CMPs on each association end holds an object of the appropriate link class as a private member.

- Association specific getters and setters in the bean implementations and remote interfaces. Two types of methods are generated:

1. User specific methods — the methods an EJB developer is working with.

2. Linkage internal methods — for inverse association maintenance. An EJB developer should not invoke these methods.

The generated methods depend on the association type.

For a CMP of a multi-valued association end the following methods are generated:

1. User specific methods:

```
java.util.Enumeration get<Role>()
void add<Role>(<inverse remote interface>)
void remove<Role>(<inverse remote interface>)
```

In our sample the generated methods in bean implementation (PersonalbankerBean) and its remote interface (Personalbanker) are:

```
java.util.Enumeration getCustomers()
void addCustomers(Customer)
void removeCustomers(Customer)
```

2. Linkage internal methods:

```
void secondaryAdd<Role>(<inverse remote interface>)
void secondardRemove<Role>(<inverse remote interface>)
```

In our sample the generated methods in the bean implementation (PersonalbankerBean) and its remote interface (Personalbanker) are:

```
void secondaryAddCustomers(Customer)
void secondaryRemoveCustomers(Customer)
```

For a CMP of a single-valued association end holding the foreign key, the following methods are generated:

1. User specific methods

```
<inverse remote interface> get<Role>()
void set<Role>(<inverse remote interface>)
```

In our sample the generated methods in bean implementation (CustomerBean) and its remote interface (Customer) are:

```
Personalbanker getPersonalbanker()
void setPersonalbanker(Personalbanker)
```

2. Linkage internal methods

```
void secondarySet<Role>(<inverse remote interface>)
void privateSet<inverse>Key(<inverse>Key)
```

In our sample the generated methods in bean implementation (CustomerBean) and its remote interface (Customer) are:

```
void secondarySetPersonalbanker(Personalbanker)
void privateSetPersonalbankerKey(PersonalbankerKey)
```

- The foreign key field(s) as CMP field(s) in the bean implementation which holds the foreign key:

```
public <type> <role>_foreignKeyFieldName;
```

In our sample the following field is generated in the CustomerBean class:

```
public java.lang.String personalbanker_bankerId;
```

The foreign key field is not visible in the Properties panel of Customer. Instead of the foreign key field, an association icon for the personalbanker role is shown. However, the foreign key field will be added in the deployment descriptor.

- An additional finder method in the remote interface of the bean's home holding the foreign key.

In our sample the following method is propagated to the CustomerHome remote interface:

```
Enumeration findCustomersByPersonalbanker(PersonalbankerKey inKey)
```

The generated link class `PersonalbankerToCustomersLink` calls `CustomerHome.findCustomerByPersonalbanker(PersonalbankerKey)` to get the personalbanker's customer enumeration.

We do not need to declare an additional method in the home remote interface of the inverse bean: the generated link class invokes the default method `findByPrimaryKey` to resolve a foreign key.

In our sample the `CustomerToPersonalbankerLink` calls `PersonalbankerHome.findByPrimaryKey(PersonalbankerKey)` to get the personalbanker reference of a customer. The link objects gets the foreign key field (personalbanker_bankerId) from its bean owner (CustomerBean).

In Figure 31, we summarize the association solution for the one-to-many relationship PersonalbankerToCustomer. The figure includes the components (link classes, bean implementations) involved, the home interfaces with the relevant association methods, the user specific accessor methods in the bean implementations, and the foreign key field at the single-valued end of the relation.

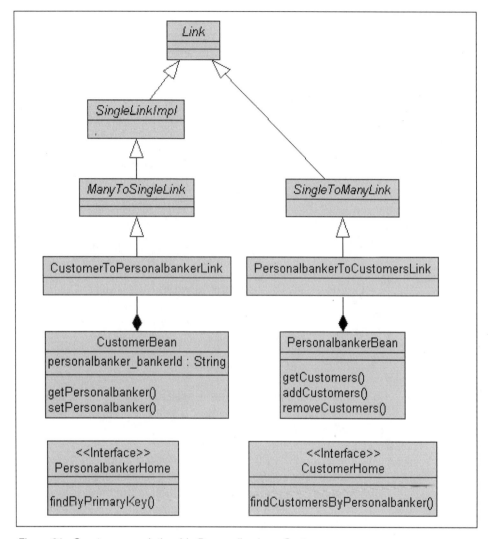

Figure 31. One-to-many relationship Personalbanker - Customer

7.2.4 Inverse association maintenance implementation

VisualAge for Java Enterprise Edition Version 3.02 supports object-level referential-integrity for associations within transactions. Each association has two ends. Changing one association end automatically maintains the inverse association side.

A major design decision of the new association solution was to enable inverse association maintenance without recursive method invocation, which means to prevent invoking a method of a beans that is already in the program stack. For example, beanA calls beanB, beanB calls (recursively) beanA. Such a solution would require bean reentrancy (selecting the Reentrant check box in the CMP Properties panel). Otherwise, a BeanNotReentrantException would be thrown.

Obviously, inverse association maintenance with reentrancy causes more method invocations, but has a simpler remote interface.

Implementing the inverse association maintenance without CMP reentrancy gives less method calls, but has another drawback: additional (linkage internal) methods in the bean implementation and its remote interface.

We describe the inverse association maintenance implementation based on the following use case:

- A customer (custA) changes his Personalbanker (from bankerA to bankerB)
- One-to-many relationship between Personalbanker and Customer

The use case can proceed in two ways:

- custA.setPersonalbanker(bankerB) or
- bankerB.addCustomers(custA)

In Figure 32, we illustrate the message flow between the CMP implementation when invoking the setter of the bean on the single-valued association end.

The interaction diagram is simplified: no distributed objects, no bean internal. A CustomerBean object (custA) holds a link object of class CustomerToPersonalbankerLink, which is the link for the single-valued end of the association. The setter of CustomerBean delegates the relationship maintenance to the link class. CustomerToPersonalbankerLink then:

- Calls bankerA.secondaryRemoveCustomers to remove the old relation on the inverse end.
- Calls bankerB.secondaryAddCustomers to update the new relation on the inverse end.
- Updates its own single-valued member (bankerB).
- Calls custA.privateSetPersonalbankerKey to update the foreign key field(s) in the bean.

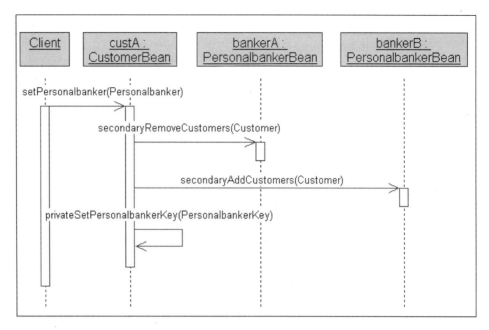

Figure 32. Interaction Diagram for Customer.setPersonalbanker (simplified)

In Figure 33, we show the message flow between the CMP implementations when invoking the add method of the bean on the multi-valued association end.

The interaction diagram is simplified: no distributed objects, no bean internal. A PersonalbankerBean object (bankerB) holds a link object of class PersonalbankerToCustomersLink, which is the link for the multi-valued end of the association. The add method of PersonalbankerBean delegates the relationship maintenance to the link class. PersonalbankerToCustomersLink then:

- Calls custA.setPersonalbanker with a null parameter to remove the old relation on the inverse end. The custA object delegates the association maintenance to its link object (class CustomerToPersonalLink) which is the link for the single-valued end of the association. CustomerToPersonalLink calls bankerA.secondaryRemoveCustomer to remove the custA object reference from the member list. CustomerToPersonalLink then sets its own member to null, which means custA has (temporary) no banker relation.

- Calls custA.secondarySetPersonalbanker to update the member on the inverse association end, which means the link object of custA now holds a reference to bankerB.

- Adds the custA object to its own member list.
- Calls `custA.privateSetPersonalbankerKey` to update the foreign key field(s) in the bean.

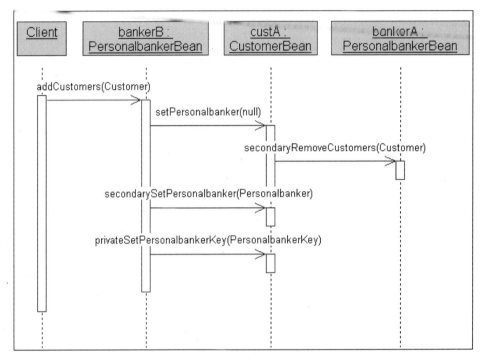

Figure 33. Interaction Diagram for Personalbanker.addCustomers (simplified)

7.3 Association developer and user responsibilities

This section describes the source code which is written by the EJB developer and some association usage issues.

7.3.1 Implementation of ejbCreate and ejbPostCreate methods

The link solution of VAJ 3.02 does not generate association-specific source for ejbCreate and ejbPostCreate methods. The EJB developer has to write the code manually.

When creating a CMP with a required (mandatory) role association maintenance has to be done during bean creation. Obviously, the role reference is passed as an argument in the creation methods (ejbCreate / ejbPostCreate).

For maintaining the other end of an association, the link class passes the ejbObject reference of the source bean when invoking the inverse setter (secondaryAdd/Remove for many-valued ends and secondarySet for single-valued ends).

The earliest point in time an EJB has access to its ejbObject reference is the postCreate method. Therefore, association maintenance has to be part of ejbPostCreate.

If the CMP holds the foreign key of a required role, the foreign key field(s) have to be set before the ejbCreate method exits. Otherwise, database exceptions can result as NULLS are written to nonNULLable columns.

In a one-to-many relationship the foreign key is always held by the single-valued end. In a one-to-one relationship, the EJB developer can define, in the Association Editor, which end of the association should hold the foreign key.

Figure 34 shows the ejbCreate / ejbPostCreate pattern for a required foreign key holder CMP.

```
public void ejbCreate(EJBObject role, ...) {
    ...
    privateSet Role Key((Role Key) role.getPrimaryKey());
}
public void ejbPostCreate(EJBObject role, ...) {
    ...
    privatSet Role Key(null);
    set Role (role);
}
```

Figure 34. ejbCreate / ejbPostCreate pattern for foreign key holder CMPs

The call to set the foreign key to null in ejbPostCreate is a necessary prerequisite to the correct functioning of the setRole call.

Figure 35 shows the ejbCreate / ejbPostCreate pattern for a non foreign key holder CMP.

```
public void ejbCreate(EJBObject role, ...) {
   ...
}
public void ejbPostCreate(EJBObject role, ...) {
   ...
   set^Role (role);
}
```

Figure 35. ejbCreate / ejbPostCreate pattern for no foreign key holder CMPs

Next, we describe a concrete usage of the ejbCreate / ejbPostCreate pattern for a one-to-many relationship. An Account object holds the required foreign key (CustomerKey) of the other association end (Customer). See Figure 36.

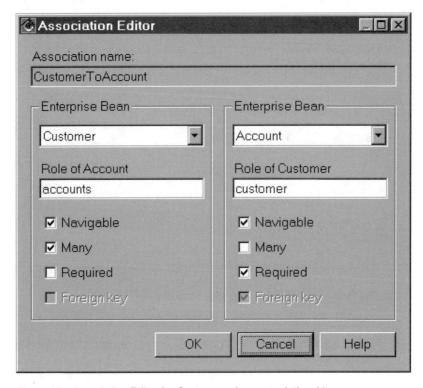

Figure 36. Association Editor for Customer - Account relationship

Figure 37 and Figure 38 show the code snippet for *AccountBean.ejbCreate(..)* and *AccountBean.ejbPostCreate(..)*.

```
public void ejbCreate(String argAccountId, Customer argCustomer)
throws javax.ejb.CreateException, java.rmi.RemoteException {
  _initLinks();
  privateSetCustomerKey((CustomerKey)
  argCustomer.getPrimaryKey());
  // All CMP fields should be initialized here.
  accountId = argAccountId;
  balance = new java.math.BigDecimal(0);
}
```

Figure 37. Code snippet for AccountBean.ejbCreate

```
public void ejbPostCreate(String argAccountId, Customer argCustomer)
throws java.rmi.RemoteException {
  privateSetCustomerKey(null);
  setCustomer(argCustomer);
}
```

Figure 38. Code snippet for AccountBean.ejbPostCreate

Finally we have to add the customized create method to the AccountHome interface.

Now we describe a concrete usage of the second ejbCreate / ejbPostCreate pattern (non foreign key holder CMP). An Employee object has a required (mandatory) Workstation role, that is, each employee use a workstation. The foreign key (EmployeeKey) is held by the other association end (Workstation). See Figure 39.

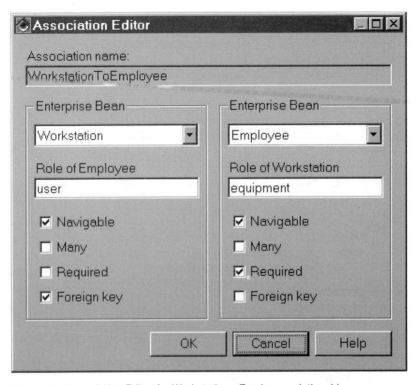

Figure 39. Association Editor for Workstation - Employee relationship

Figure 40 and Figure 41 show the code snippet for
EmployeeBean.ejbCreate(..) and *EmployeeBean.ejbPostCreate(..)*.

```
public void ejbCreate(String argEmployeeId, String argName,
Workstation argWorkstation) throws javax.ejb.CreateException,
java.rmi.RemoteException {
    _initLinks();
    // All CMP fields should be initialized here.
    employeeId = argEmployeeId;
    name = argName;
}
```

Figure 40. Code snippet for EmployeeBean.ejbCreate

The ejbcreate method has the Workstation argument in its signature, but no
additional method invocation is required. The _initLinks() call has been
included from VAJ tooling support during CMP creation time.

```
public void ejbPostCreate(String argEmployeeId, String argName,
Workstation argWorkstation) throws java.rmi.RemoteException {
   setEquipment(argWorkstation);
}
```

Figure 41. Code snippet for EmployeeBean.ejbPostCreate

Finally, we have to add the customized create method to the EmployeeHome
interface.

7.3.2 Delete cascading

Composition is a form of aggregation, with strong ownership and coincident
lifetime as part of the whole. Parts may be created after the composite itself,
but once created they live and die with it. Such parts can also be explicitly
removed before the death of the composite.

Any deletion of the whole is considered to cascade to the parts. This
cascading delete is often considered to be a defining part of composition, but
it is implied by any role with a 1..1 multiplicity; if you want to delete a
Customer, for instance, you must cascade that delete to Accounts.

The Association support of VisualAge for Java, 3.02 neither actively supports
composition nor delete cascading.

We describe the current delete behavior based on a Customer - Account
sample (see Figure 42).

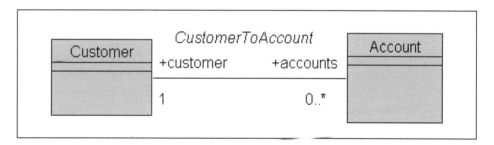

Figure 42. Class Diagram Customer - Account relationship

Figure 36 on page 74 shows the Association Editor for the one-to-many
association. The customer role in Account is required (mandatory): each
account has a customer. An Account holds the foreign key
(customer_customerId).

Figure 43 illustrates the current delete implementation of a Customer.

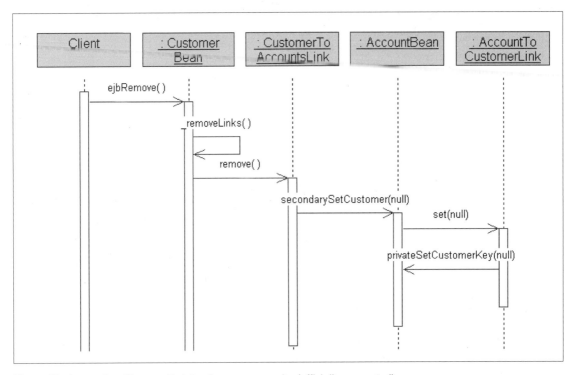

Figure 43. Interaction Diagram: Delete of a non composite (officially supported)

The Association framework tries to nullify the customer role reference and the foreign key field (customer_customerId) in AccountBean. Delete of a customer throws an exception 'SQL0532N A parent row cannot be deleted because the relationship restricts the deletion'.

We could enforce a cascade delete with a database constraint in table Account, but this would prevent association maintenance: Account could have other associations which have to be propagated to the other association ends before an account dies.

We have to ensure that all customer's accounts have been removed before we remove the customer.

Official solution for deleted cascading
We have to explicitly remove all the customer's accounts before we delete the customer. Obviously we would delete the accounts of a customer in Customer.ejbRemove(), before calling _removeLinks(). But the delete of an account from within CustomerBean throws a BeanNotReentrantException

unless we would allow recursive method invocation by selecting the Reentrant check box in the Customer Properties panel. We do not want to set Customer as reentrant and will instead delete the customer's accounts outside CustomerBean in a Session Facade (BusinessProcessBean). See Figure 44 and Figure 45.

```
public void removeCustomer(String customerId) throws
java.rmi.RemoteException, javax.ejb.FinderException,
javax.ejb.RemoveException {
    Customer customerToRemove = getCustomer(customerId);
    removeAllAccountsOfCustomer(customerToRemove);
    customerToRemove.remove();
}
```

Figure 44. BusinessProcessBean.removeCustomer(String)

```
private void removeAllAccountsOfCustomer(Customer customer) throws
RemoteException, javax.ejb.FinderException, javax.ejb.RemoveException {
    java.util.Enumeration accountEnum = customer.getAccounts();
    while(accountEnum.hasMoreElements()) {
        java.rmi.Remote remoteObject = (java.rmi.Remote)
            accountEnum.nextElement();
        Account account = (Account)
            javax.rmi.PortableRemoteObject.narrow(remoteObject,
            Account.class);
        account.remove();
    }
}
```

Figure 45. BusinessProcessBean.removeAllAccountsOfCustomer(Customer)

Unofficial solution for deleted cascading

VisualAge for Java 3.02 does not define an association of type Composition in the Association Editor. However, the abstract class Link which is the base class of all generated concrete links enables delete cascading via beComposite(). The behavior of a concrete Link class depends on the composite flag setting of the base class. Figure 43 illustrates the delete behavior of a non composite association. Figure 46 shows the message flow when deleting a composite.

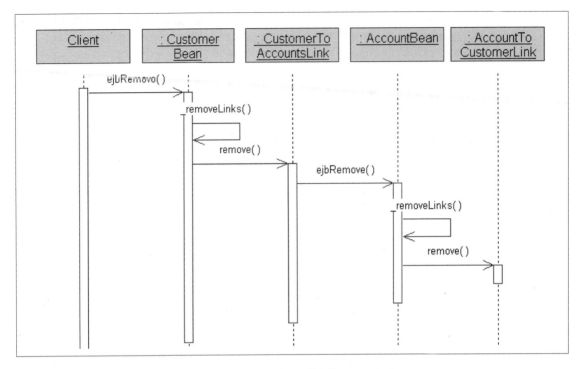

Figure 46. Interaction Diagram: Delete of a composite (not officially supported)

The delete of a composite (Customer) is cascaded to the parts (Account). To enable delete cascade we set the composite flag for CustomerToAddressLink in two CustomerBean methods: ejbCreate and ejbLoad (see Figure 47 and Figure 48).

```
public void ejbCreate(java.lang.String argCustomerId, String argName)
throws javax.ejb.CreateException, java.rmi.RemoteException {
    _initLinks();
    ((CustomerToAddressLink) getAddressLink()).beComposite();
    // All CMP fields should be initialized here.
    customerId = argCustomerId;
    name = argName;
}
```

Figure 47. Composite setter for CustomerToAddressLink in ejbcreate

```
public void ejbLoad() throws java.rmi.RemoteException {
    _initLinks();
    ((CustomerToAddressLink) getAddressLink()).beComposite();
}
```

Figure 48. Composite setter for CustomerToAddressLink in ejbLoad

The current implementation of a composite remove requires reentrancy of the link owner's bean, because of recursive method invocations. In our sample the Reentrant check box in the Customer's Properties panel has to be selected (see Figure 49).

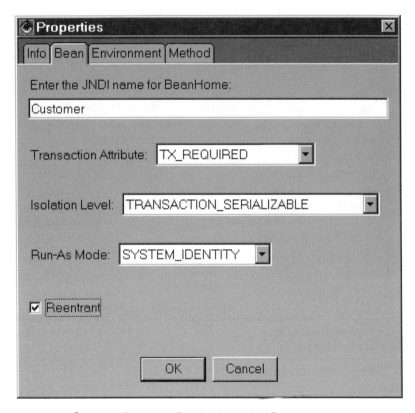

Figure 49. Customer Properties Panel with checked Reentrant

7.3.3 Use of associations with required roles

For some of the generated methods in an association with a required role unexpected behavior occurs. They should never be invoked. This chapter addresses the critical methods.

7.3.3.1 One-to-many with a required role

We are discussing the issues for a one-to-many association with a required role based on the Customer - Account relation (see Figure 36 on page 74). Customer role is required in Account. This means that an Account must have a customer. The Account implementation (AccountBean) holds the foreign key field (customer_customorld), which cannot be null.

Role is part of the primary key

As long as the role is part of the primary key, it is illegal to call any operations on the remote interface of the two associated beans that will try to update the foreign key field(s). Updating of the foreign key field(s) would mean changing the OID of the bean, because the foreign key is part of the primary key. In our example, the critical methods *not* to be invoked are:

- `Account.setCustomer(Account)`
- `Customer.addAccounts(Account)`
- `Customer.removeAccounts(Account)`

The only way to create an account of a customer is via `AccountHome.create(Customer, ...)` and the only way to remove one is via `Account.remove()` or `AccountHome.remove(Account)`. An account cannot be transferred to another customer. Remove of a customer includes removing of the customer's accounts (delete cascading). The tools do not support delete cascading. For work-arounds, see 7.3.2, "Delete cascading" on page 77.

In Table 1, we summarize the usage of a one-to-many relationship (Customer - Account) with a required role which is part of the primary key. We take into account only the user specific association maintenance methods. The linkage internal methods in the remote interfaces of the two associated beans are not relevant in our discussion. For a detailed discussion, see 7.2, "Description of the association solution" on page 64.

Table 1. Customer - Account relation (customer role is part account key)

method invocations [use cases]	create accnt	delete accnt	transf accnt
anAccountHome.create(customerA, accountId) [create accountA for customerA]	OK [a]		
accountA.remove() [delete accountA]		OK	
anAccountHome.remove(accountA) [delete accountA via AccountHome]		OK	
customerB.removeAccounts(accountA) [remove accountA from member list of customerB]		NO [b]	

method invocations [use cases]	create accnt	delete accnt	transf accnt
customerB.addAccounts(accountA) [transfer accountA to customerB from multi-valued association end]			NO [c]
accountA.setCustomer(customerB) [transfer accountA to customerB from single-valued association end]			NO [c]
customerA.remove() [d]			

a. User written code (see 7.3.1, "Implementation of ejbCreate and ejb-PostCreate methods" on page 72).
b. Tries to set primary key (or part of it) to null.
c. It is illegal to call any operation on the remote interface of the two associated beans that will try to update the foreign key fields (which are part of the primary key).
d. Delete cascading (removing customerA's accounts) is not supported from the tools. For work-arounds, see 7.3.2, "Delete cascading" on page 77.

A one-to-many relationship with a required role which is part of the primary key is an aggregation / composition (whole/part). A part (Account) cannot changed its whole (Customer) and ties with the whole.

Role is not part of the primary key
When the role is not part of the primary key the association solution has less method invocation restrictions: changing the foreign key does not change the OID of the bean. In our example the critical methods not to be invoked are: `Account.setCustomer(null)` and `Customer.removeAccounts(Account)`.

In contrast to the previous scenario (role is part of the primary key) an account could be transferred to another customer from a primary, foreign key point of view. However, if the Customer - Account relation is an aggregation / composition, `Account.setCustomer(Customer)` or `Customer.addAccounts(Account)` should never be invoked.

In Table 2, we summarize the usage of a one-to-many relationship (Customer - Account) with a required role which is not part of the primary key. We take into account only the user specific association maintenance methods. The linkage internal methods in the remote interfaces of the two associated beans are not relevant in our discussion. For a detailed discussion, see 7.2, "Description of the association solution" on page 64.

Table 2. Customer - Account relation (customer role is not part account key)

method invocations [use cases]	create accnt	delete accnt	transf accnt
anAccountHome.create(customerA, accountId) [create aooountA for customerA]	OK [a]		
accountA.remove() [delete accountA]		OK	
anAccountHome.remove(accountA) [delete accountA via AccountHome]		OK	
customerB.removeAccounts(accountA) [remove accountA from member list of customerB]		NO [b]	
customerB.addAccounts(accountA) [transfer accountA to customerB from multi-valued association end]			OK [c]
accountA.setCustomer(customerB) [transfer accountA to customerB from single-valued association end]			OK [c] [d]
customerA.remove() [e]			

a. User written code (see 7.3.1, "Implementation of ejbCreate and ejb-PostCreate methods" on page 72).

b. Tries to set the foreign key field (customerId) to null. Because the customer role in Account is mandatory (required) an SQL0407N exception is thrown ("Assignment of a NULL value to a NOT NULL column is not allowed").

c. If the Customer - Acount relationship is a composition (whole/part) this method should not to be invoked (a part cannot change its whole).

d. If the customerB reference is null an SQL0407N exception is thrown (rational see footnote b).

e. Delete cascading (removing customerA's accounts) is not supported from the tools. For work-arounds, see 7.3.2, "Delete cascading" on page 77.

7.3.3.2 One-to-one with a required role

We are discussing the issues for a one-to-one association with a required role based on the Customer - Address relation (see Figure 50). Customer role is required in Address. This means that an address must have a customer. The Address implementation (AddressBean) holds the foreign key field (customer_customerId), which cannot be null.

Figure 50. Association Editor for Customer - Address relation

Role is part of the primary key

In our sample we decide to make the foreign key of Customer to the primary key of Address. This means that the foreign key field customer_customerId in AddressBean is the primary key of Address.

As long as the role is part of the primary key, it is illegal to call any operations on the remote interface of the two associated beans that will try to update the foreign key field(s). Updating of the foreign key field(s) would mean: changing the OID of the bean, because the foreign key is part of the primary key.

In our sample the critical methods *not* to be invoked are:
`Customer.setAddress(Address)` and `Address.setCustomer(Customer)`. The only way to create an address of a customer is via `AddressHome.create(Customer, ...)` and the only way to remove one is via `Address.remove()` or `AddressHome.remove(Address)`. An address cannot be transferred to another customer. Remove of a customer includes removing his address (delete cascading). The tools do not support delete cascading. For work-arounds, see 7.3.2, "Delete cascading" on page 77.

In Table 3, we summarize the usage of a one-to-one relationship (Customer - Address) with a required role which is (part of) the primary key. We take into account only the user specific association maintenance methods. The linkage internal methods in the remote interfaces of the two associated beans are not relevant in our discussion. For a detailed discussion, see 7.2, "Description of the association solution" on page 04.

Table 3. Customer - Address relation (customer role is primary key of address)

method invocations [use cases]	create addr	delete addr	transf addr
anAddressHome.create(customerA) [create addressA for customerA]	OK [a]		
addressA.remove() [delete addressA]		OK [b]	
anAddressHome.remove(addressA) [delete addressA via AddressHome]		OK [b]	
customerB.setAddress(addressA) [transfer addressA to customerB]			NO [c]
addressA.setCustomer(customerB) [transfer addressA to customerB]			NO [c]
customerA.remove() [d]			

a. User written code (see 7.3.1, "Implementation of ejbCreate and ejb-PostCreate methods" on page 72).

b. From a primary / foreign key perspective this is not an issue. However we have defined the address role in Customer as required. Deleting the address of a customer would violate the multiplicity rule.

c. It is illegal to call any operation on the remote interface of the two associated beans that will try to update the foreign key field which is (part of) the primary key.

d. Delete cascading (removing customerA's address) is not supported from the tools. For work-arounds, see 7.3.2, "Delete cascading" on page 77.

Role is not part of the primary key

When the role is not part of the primary key the association solution has less method invocation restrictions: changing the foreign key does not change the OID of the bean. In our example, the critical method not to invoke is:

```
Address.setCustomer(null).
```

In contrast to the previous scenario (role is part of the primary key) an address could be transferred to another customer from a primary, foreign key point of view. However, if the Customer - Address relation is an aggregation / composition `Address.setCustomer(Customer)` or `Customer.setAddress(Address)` should never be invoked.

In Table 4, we summarize the usage of a one-to-one relationship (Customer - Address) with a required role which is not part of the primary key. We take into account only the user specific association maintenance methods. The linkage internal methods in the remote interfaces of the two associated beans are not relevant in our discussion. For a detailed discussion, see 7.2, "Description of the association solution" on page 64.

Table 4. Customer - Address relation (customer role is not part of address key)

method invocations [use cases]	create addr	delete addr	transf addr
anAddressHome.create(customerA, ...) [create addressA for customerA]	OK [a]		
addressA.remove() [delete addressA]		OK [b]	
anAddressHome.remove(addressA) [delete addressA via AddressHome]		OK [b]	
customerB.setAddress(addressA) [transfer addressA to customerB]			OK [c]
addressA.setCustomer(customerB) [transfer addressA to customerB]			OK [c d]
customerA.remove() [e]			

a. User written code (see 7.3.1, "Implementation of ejbCreate and ejb-PostCreate methods" on page 72).

b. From a technical primary, foreign key perspective this is not an issue. However we have defined the address role in Customer as required. Deleting the address of a customer would violate the multiplicity rule.

c. If the Customer - Address relationship is a composition (whole/part) this method should not to be invoked (a part cannot change its whole).

d. If the customerB reference is null an SQL0407N exception is thrown ("Assignment of a NULL value to a NOT NULL column is not allow"). Customer role in Address is required.

e. Delete cascading (removing customerA's address) is not supported from the tools. For work-arounds, see 7.3.2, "Delete cascading" on page 77.

7.3.4 Many-to-many relationships

Many-to-many relationships are not fully supported. Many-to-many associations have to be handled as two 1:M associations to an intermediary object. This intermediate object must then be mapped to an intermediary table.

In this section we describe the development of a Many-to-many relationship Employee - Skill (see Figure 51).

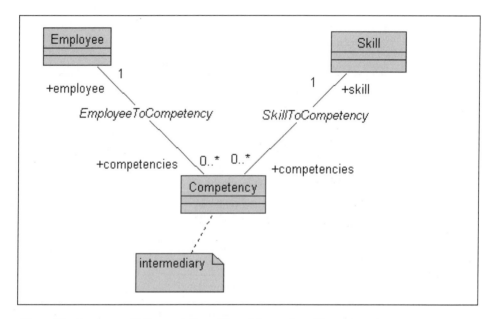

Figure 51. Employee - Skill association with an intermediary (Competency)

The intermediary EJB is Competency. The primary key for Competency is composed of the primary keys of Employee and Skill.

We explore the development of the Competency EJB and the two relationships step by step:

- We create the Competency as a CMP with the SmartGuide. We don't define the primary key at this time. A warning panel appears (Enterprise bean has no key fields). We ignore the warning.

- We define the first one-to-many relationship between Employee and Competency (see Figure 52).

The characteristics of the employee role (not many-valued, both required and navigable, holds the foreign key) are a prerequisite for adding the employee role to the Competency key in a later development step.

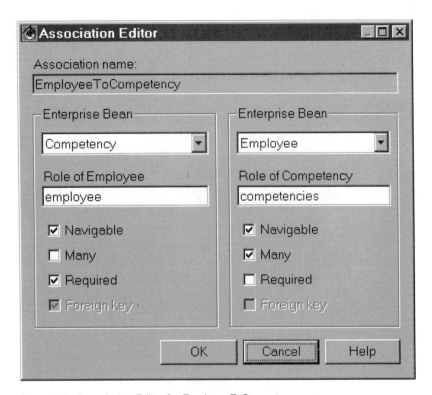

Figure 52. Association Editor for EmployeeToCompetency

- We define the second one-to-many relationship between Skill and Competency (see Figure 53).

  The characteristics of the skill role (not many-valued, both required and navigable, holds the foreign key) are a prerequisite for adding the skill role to the Competency key in a later development step.

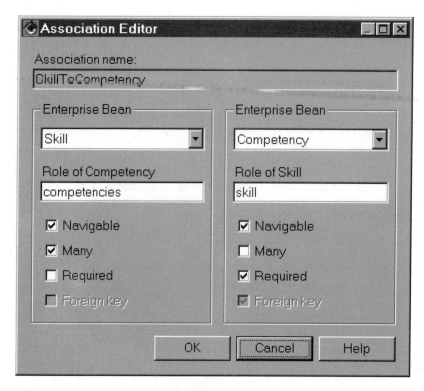

Figure 53. Association Editor for EmployeeToCompetency

- In the next step, we define the primary key for Competency. In the Properties panel of Competency :

  - Select (right-click) the employee role icon, and choose **Add Role To Key** in the pop-up. This adds the key field of Employee (employeeId) to both the CompetencyKey and CompetencyBean (employee_employeeId).

  - Select (right-click) the skill role icon, and choose **Add Role To Key** in the pop-up. This adds the key field of Skill (skillId) to both the CompetencyKey and CompetencyBean (skill_skillId).

  The primary key of Competency is now composed of the two foreign keys (Employee, Skill). Figure 54 illustrates the Properties panel after adding the role keys.

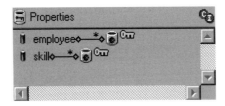

Figure 54. Properties Panel of Competency after adding the role keys

- To create an Employee - Skill relationship (that means, to create a new Competency object) we have to change the ejbCreate and ejbPostCreate methods of the Competency class. The ejbCreate and ejbPostCreate methods, that VisualAge generated when we created the Competency, have no arguments. We delete both methods and create another method pair (see Figure 55 and Figure 56). The new ejbCreate and ejbPostCreate methods both have the Employee and Skill remote interface as parameters.

```
public void ejbCreate(Employee argEmployee, Skill argSkill) throws
javax.ejb.CreateException, java.rmi.RemoteException {
   _initLinks();
   privateSetEmployeeKey((EmployeeKey) argEmployee.getPrimaryKey());
   privateSetSkillKey((SkillKey) argSkill.getPrimaryKey());
   // All CMP fields should be initialized here.
}
```

Figure 55. Method implementation for CompetencyBean.ejbCreate

```
public void ejbPostCreate(Employee argEmployee, Skill argSkill, int
argLevel) throws java.rmi.RemoteException {
   privateSetEmployeeKey(null);
   privateSetSkillKey(null);
   setEmployee(argEmployee);
   setSkill(argSkill);
}
```

Figure 56. Method implementation for CompetencyBean.ejbPostCreate

A detailed description of the association-specific code statements in ejbCreate and ejbPost can be found in 7.3.1, "Implementation of ejbCreate and ejbPostCreate methods" on page 72.

We add the ejbCreate method to the EJB Home interface (CompetencyHome).

- When deleting an Employee or Skill object we have to ensure that all intermediary members (objects of type Competency in our example) are deleted as well

The two created one-to-many associations to the intermediary Competency (EmployeeToCompetency, SkillToCompetency) are special association types: aggregation / composition. With composition, the part object (for example, Competency) may belong to only one whole (for example, Employee); further, the parts are usually expected to live and die with the whole. Any deletion of the whole is considered to cascade to the parts. VisualAge for Java 3.02 does not support aggregation / composition.

There are two solutions to enforce delete cascading (see 7.3.2, "Delete cascading" on page 77).

- We have already mentioned that the Competency class has a compound primary key based on the Employee and Skill key (employee and skill roles both are required in Competency). Some of the generated association setters in the CMPs tries to change the identity of the Competency object which would lead to an unexpected behavior. The critical methods not to be invoked are:

  - Employee.addCompetencies(Competency)
  - Employee.removeCompetencies(Competency)
  - Skill.addCompetencies(Competency)
  - Skill.removeCompetencies(Competency)
  - Competency.setEmployee(Employee)
  - Competency.setSkill(Skill)

For a detailed description see 7.3.3, "Use of associations with required roles" on page 81 and Table 1 on page 82.

Next, we are implementing some use cases for the Employee - Skill association with a Session EJB. To ensure that each use case is run within a unit-of-work, we set the transaction attribute of the session bean to TX_REQUIRED.

In Figure 57, we demonstrate the session source for creating a competency.

```
public void createCompeteny(String employeeId, String skillId) throws
java.rmi.RemoteException, javax.ejb.CreateException,
javax.ejb.FinderException {
   Employee employee = getEmployee(employeeId);
   Skill skill = getSkill(skillId);
   getCompetencyHome().create(employee, skill);
}
```

Figure 57. Create a competency

In Figure 58, we show how to get the skill descriptions of an employee.

```
public java.util.Vector getSkillDescriptionsOfEmployee(String
employeeId) throws RemoteException, javax.ejb.FinderException {
   Employee employee = getEmployee(employeeId);
   java.util.Enumeration competencyEnum = employee.getCompetencies();
   java.util.Vector skillDescriptions = new java.util.Vector();
   while(competencyEnum.hasMoreElements()) {
      java.rmi.Remote remoteObject =
         (java.rmi.Remote) competencyEnum.nextElement();
      Competency competency = (Competency)
         javax.rmi.PortableRemoteObject.narrow(remoteObject,
         Competency.class);
      skillDescriptions.addElement(competency.getSkill().
      getDescription());
   }
   return skillDescriptions;
}
```

Figure 58. Get skill descriptions of an employee

In Figure 59, we illustrate the delete of an employee and his competencies.
We have to explicitly remove the employee's competencies before the delete
of the employee, because we have not set the composite flag in the
EmployeeToCompetenciesLink object (see 7.3.2, "Delete cascading" on page
77, and "Official solution for deleted cascading" on page 78).

```
public void removeEmployee(String employeeId) throws
java.rmi.RemoteException, javax.ejb.FinderException,
javax.ejb.RemoveException {
      Employee employee = getEmployee(employeeId);
      removeEmployeeCompetencies(employeeId);
      employee.remove();
}
```

Figure 59. Delete an employee

In Figure 60, we show the code to delete the skill and its associated competencies. We do not have to explicitly remove the competencies, because we have set the composite flag in the SkillToCompetenciesLink object (see 7.3.2, "Delete cascading" on page 77 and "Unofficial solution for deleted cascading" on page 79).

```
public void removeSkill(String skillId) throws
java.rmi.RemoteException, javax.ejb.FinderException,
javax.ejb.RemoveException {
      Skill skill = getSkill(skillId);
      skill.remove();
}
```

Figure 60. Delete a skill

7.4 Hints and tips

In this section we list a few hints and tips for association developers.

7.4.1 Usage of the multi-valued getters

The system workload caused by the invocation of a multi-valued getter depends on the transaction context.

If the getter is called within a transaction context, the first five members are activated and initialized from the database. Other members are activated and hydrated from the persistent store (in chunks of five elements) by iterating the enumerator within the same transaction.

If the getter is called outside of a transaction context, the returned enumerator includes all member elements, but the members are not activated yet. A member will be activated by a method call.

When we are developing an application, we have to be aware of the implication of the multi-valued getters, especially if we have a high number of elements. For a detailed discussion and alternatives see Chapter 8, "Collections" on page 101.

7.4.2 Associations with subtypes

In this section, we describe the one-to-many sample Customer - Account. Account is an 'abstract' CMP and has concrete subtypes (SavingsAccount, CheckingAccount). The EJB inheritance support of VisualAge for Java supports polymorphic homes, which means AccountHome can identify and instantiate account subtypes. The aim of this chapter is to describe how the caller of Customer.getAccounts(), which returns an enumeration of account subtypes, can evaluate the concrete account types (see Figure 61).

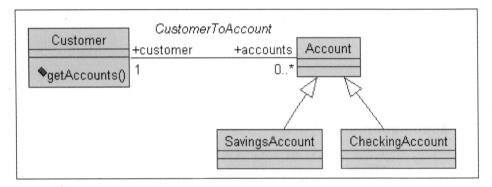

Figure 61. Customer - Account relation with account subtypes

In general, it is not possible in CORBA to ask a remote object for its most derived type. We can ask if it supports a specific type by calling PortableRemoteObject.narrow(). In Figure 62, we show the source of a narrow helper method.

```
private Object tryNarrow(java.rmi.Remote remoteObject, Class cls) {
    try {
        return javax.rmi.PortableRemoteObject.narrow(remoteObject, cls);
    }
    catch(ClassCastException castExcept) {
        return remoteObject;
    }
}
```

Figure 62. Narrow helper method

In Figure 63 we illustrate the use of the narrow helper method.

```
public String[] getAccountIdsOfCustomer(String customerId) throws
RemoteException {
    accountEnum = getCustomer(customerId).getAccounts();
    while( accountEnum.hasMoreElements()) {
        Remote remoteObject = accountEnum.nextElement();
        if ((remoteObject = tryNarrow(remoteObject,
            SavingsAccount.class)) instanceof SavingsAccount {
            //type is a savings account
        }
        else if ((remoteObject = tryNarrow(remoteObject,
            CheckingAccount.class)) instanceof CheckingAccount {
            //type is a checking account
        }
        ...
    }
}
```

Figure 63. Source using the narrow helper method

7.5 Association deployment

In this section we discuss the deployment of EJBs with associations to different Application Servers.

7.5.1 Deployment descriptor

VisualAge for Java adds the foreign key fields as container-managed fields to the deployment descriptor (see 7.2, "Description of the association solution" on page 64).

The deployment descriptor contains the generated association specific remote interface methods (beans and homes).

A description of the association mapping (mapping the foreign keys to database fields) can be found in the official documentation and is not addressed in this redbook.

7.5.2 Deployment on WebSphere Advanced Edition

Typically, an EJB developer has to provide finder logic for each finder method (other than the findByPrimaryKey method) contained in the home interface of an entity bean with CMP. When deploying on WebSphere Advanced the EJB developer does not have to provide the finder logic for the association specific methods. The tools support delivers the appropriate SQL statement.

We have tested the association solution deployment on IBM WebSphere Advanced Edition 3.02.

7.5.3 Deployment on WebSphere Enterprise Edition (CB)

Associations are deployed on IBM WebSphere Application Server Enterprise Edition Component Broker 3.0.2.1 (Service Pack 3).

As mentioned above when developing associations, VisualAge for Java automatically creates additional CMP fields that correspond to foreign keys. CB does not currently support NULL values for primitive types, for example java.lang.Integer and java.lang.Long. Because the foreign key of an optional (non required) role can be NULL, we have to ensure that the primary key field(s) of the inverse bean is (are) of type String. A String can be null in CB.

In our one-to-many sample PersonalbankerToCustomer, where the personalbanker role in Customer is optional (see Figure 30 on page 66), the primary key field of Personalbanker (bankerId) has to be a String.

7.5.4 Deployment on non WebSphere application servers

The association solution is built on top of the EJB specifications. Associations built with VisualAge for Java should be portable to any EJB 1.0 compliant application server. We have not tested the association deployment on non WebSphere application servers.

7.5.5 Runtime requirements

To deploy Jar files containing associations, we copy ivjejb302.jar from VisualAge for Java's eab\runtime30 directory to the application server and client machines. We set our server and client CLASSPATH to point to this jar file.

7.6 Performance impacts

In this section we discuss the influence associations may have on performance.

7.6.1 Inverse association maintenance

A major enhancement of the association solution of VisualAge for Java 3.02 is association integrity within a transactions (inverse association maintenance).

But this association integrity has its price. For the inverse association maintenance additional remote methods are invoked (for a detailed description see 7.2.4, "Inverse association maintenance implementation" on page 69).

As we illustrated in the referenced section, updating a one-to-many association from the single-valued end causes less additional remote method invocations (2) for the inverse association maintenance as does updating the relationship from the multi-valued end (4).

If both CMPs involved in an association are deployed on the same application server process, the in-process optimization of WebSphere can decrease the method invocation overhead.

7.6.2 Maintaining association members

The association solution supports lazy member initialization. This means, for example, the accounts of a customer are activated and loaded from the database when Customer.getAccounts() is called. The members (accounts of a customer) are not cached in the link objects.

Inverse association maintenance does not instantiate the inverse members. The EjbMemberEnumeration class which is part of the association runtime support ensures association integrity within a transaction without the need of instantiating all members before explicitly requested.

For one-to-many associations with a high number of members, the invocation of multi-valued getters can have a performance implication. See 7.4.1, "Usage of the multi-valued getters" on page 94.

7.6.3 Association method types (read-only /update)

In order to prevent an unnecessary SQL UPDATE at commitment and to get better overall performance, it is safe to mark some methods of the remote interface as const (this means read-only). We are using the enterprise bean's Properties Editor in VisualAge for Java (Method panel) and select the flag in the Control Descriptor window of the appropriate methods (see Figure 64). The current version of the Jetace deployment tools does not allow to set the const flag.

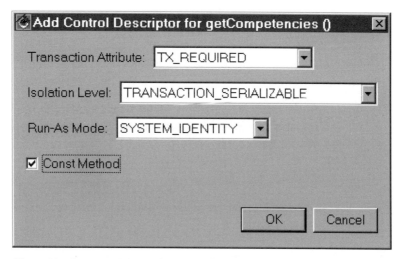

Figure 64. Const mark in the Control Descriptor

For generated association methods, the following example illustrates which methods can be marked const:

- Single-valued association end:
    - get<role>()
    - get<role>Key()
    - secondarySet<role>(<inverse remote interface>)
- Multi-valued association end:
    - get<role>()
    - add<role>(<inverse remote interface>)
    - secondaryAdd<role>(<inverse remote interface>)
    - remove<role>(<inverse remote interface>)
    - secondaryRemove<role>(<inverse remote interface>)

The only method that must be left non-const (Const Method check box not selected) is set<Role>(<inverse remote interface>) and privateSet<Role>Key(<Role>Key) on the single-valued association end. This method updates the foreign key field(s).

7.6.4 Accessing the naming service

The Association solution intensively invokes the CMP's home finders. The current implementation does neither cache the initial context reference of the naming service nor the home references. This can lead to a performance overhead.

In this section, we illustrate an enhancement in the
com.ibm.ivj.ejb.associations.links.Link class, which improves the naming
service performance.

The original source code for the Association Runtime support is available in
VisualAge for Java.

In Figure 65, we show the customized lookupTargetHome method of the Link
class. The naming service is delegated to an EJB home factory singleton. For
a detailed description of this pattern, see 10.1, "Factory for EJB Homes" on
page 149.

```
protected EJBHome lookupTargetHome(String className, Class homeClass)
throws NamingException {
    /* Delegate naming service to an EJB home factory singleton */
    try {
        return HomeFactory.getSingleton().lookupHome(className);
    }
    catch(Exception except) {
        throw new NamingException();
    }
    /*
    EJBHome home = null;
    javax.naming.InitialContext initialContext;
    java.util.Properties properties = new java.util.Properties();
    properties.put(javax.naming.Context.INITIAL_CONTEXT_FACTORY,
    contextFactoryName());
    initialContext = new javax.naming.InitialContext(properties);
    java.lang.Object obj = initialContext.lookup(className);
    home = (EJBHome) javax.rmi.PortableRemoteObject.narrow(obj,
    homeClass);
    return home;
    */
}
```

Figure 65. Customized lookupTargetHome method of the LInk class

To enable the performance improvement in the application server runtime, we
package the customized Link class in a .jar file and set this jar in the
CLASSPATH in front of the original ivjejb302.jar (see 7.5, "Association
deployment" on page 96).

Chapter 8. Collections

Most applications found on the Web, at some point, have to display information corresponding to a collection of elements. These elements can be, for example, products or bank accounts.

When they represent business objects implemented as enterprise beans, building the list of attributes by instantiating all the beans in order to get the necessary properties may not be the best solution. Another approach based on the use of the JDBC API to create this list of attributes is probably more efficient.

Making a choice is a matter of trade-offs between flexibility and maintainability versus performances, which are the subjects of this chapter.

8.1 What are collections?

By collection we mean a set of objects that satisfy given conditions. In order to retrieve these objects, a business developer working in an object oriented environment ideally would like to execute some kind of finder that is conceptually very similar to performing query on a relational database. It differs in that the finder results on a collection of objects rather than a collection of records, and the predicate is formed on the set of attributes rather than on columns in the tables.

Such capabilities are described in the CORBA's Query Service. It defines interfaces to create collections and to add, remove, and replace elements in the object space. A product such as Component Broker implements these advanced services.

Since our business logic is Implemented as enterprise beans, let us look at what the Enterprise JavaBeans specification provides to the business logic developer.

8.2 Enumerations with finders

In the Enterprise JavaBeans specification, collection of enterprise beans are retrieved by using finder methods that are declared in the bean home interface.

Currently the specification does not provide a *formal* mechanism for the Bean Provider to specify the criteria for the finder methods, nor syntax for describing the finders.

101

It is up to the container provider to specify the format of the finder method description. So, what is relevant in the enterprise bean specification is for the reader to be aware of the absence or presence of constraints imposed on container providers.

8.2.1 Finders

Finders, as described in the Enterprise JavaBeans specification, are methods defined on the bean home. They are executed with the transaction context of the caller.

8.2.1.1 Enterprise JavaBeans specification 1.0

The first version of the specification the Enterprise Bean's states that

"The return type for a *finder* method must be the enterprise Bean's remote interface type, or a collection of thereof."

And also:

"The return type of an entity finder method can be either a single enterprise bean object reference or a collection of enterprise bean object references. If there is the possibility that the finder method may find more than one enterprise bean object, the Bean developer should define the return type of the *ejbFind<METHOD>(...)* and *find<METHOD>(...)* method to be a collection.

The JDK 1.1.x type for a collection is the *java.util.Enumeration* interface, and therefore a finder method that returns a collection of enterprise bean objects must define the return type to be *java.util.Enumeration.*"

8.2.1.2 Enterprise JavaBeans specification 1.1

The new version adds the possibility to return a *java.util.Collection* instead of a *java.util.Enumeration* when targeting only containers and clients based on the Java 2 platform.

Consequences

For IBM WebSphere Advanced Edition based on the JDK 1.1, only *java.util.Enumeration* of enterprise bean remote interfaces are supported.

This implies that a client application will get access to any single attribute through remote methods calls over RMI-IIOP.

Keep in mind the performance implications during design considerations.

8.2.1.3 Using finders in IBM WebSphere Advanced Edition

IBM WebSphere Advanced Edition in combination with VisualAge for Java offers different ways to specify finder methods.

Two old style custom finders, known as SELECT and WHERE, are quite limited in their usage. They are based on a partial or complete static description of a SQL string. These solutions could not survive the introduction of enterprise bean inheritance.

In order to support new features like inheritance, they were replaced by the METHOD custom finder. A method custom finder uses a method signature in the finder helper interface instead of a static string. The developer needs to implement a new class that extends VapEJSJDBCFinderObject which provides several important helper methods to insert in WHERE clauses in multiple points in a base query string.

This new way of implementing a finder provides all the flexibility you need to create complex queries. The use of finder is the unique solution described in the Enterprise JavaBeans specification for clients that need to process a collection of enterprise beans. In IBM WebSphere Advanced Edition, the execution of a finder method returns an enumeration. It can be a greedy or lazy enumeration.

8.2.2 Greedy and lazy enumerations

Depending on the caller's transaction context, the enumeration is greedy or lazy.

8.2.2.1 Greedy mode

A finder will operate in greedy mode when called with no active transaction.

When in greedy mode, the resulting enumeration will be fully formed at the time the finder method returns. However, the elements are not yet activated. This enumeration may be passed around at will and enumerated at any point in time. There's no guarantee, however, that all members of the enumeration will still exist.

8.2.2.2 Lazy mode

In contrast, a finder will operate in lazy mode when there is an active transaction at the time the finder method is invoked. This will typically be the case, for example, if you have a session bean with its transaction attribute set to TX_REQUIRED invoking a finder.

When in lazy mode, the resulting enumeration is not fully formed when the finder method returns. The JDBC result set remains open on the server; the enumeration received by the caller will fetch members of the result set in batches from the server as you step through the enumeration.

A lazy enumeration is valid only until the transaction in which the finder was invoked commits. Attempts to use the enumeration after the transaction has committed will result in an `IllegalStateException`.

8.2.3 Coding rules

The following examples show how to program correct enterprise bean clients using entity enterprise bean finders or association getters. The session and entity beans in these examples have their transaction attribute set to TX_REQUIRED unless otherwise specified. The code examples are:

- Pure Java enterprise bean client
- Session bean client
- Pure Java enterprise bean client programming errors
- Session enterprise bean
- Session enterprise bean programming errors
- Back to Session enterprise bean correctly programmed

Pure Java enterprise bean client

In the following example in Figure 66, the finder will execute in **greedy** mode, since there is no transaction active at the time the finder was invoked.

```
...
// finder in greedy mode
Enumeration result = entityHome.findAll();
while (result.hasMoreElements()) {
    Object o = result.nextElement();
...
}
```

Figure 66. Enterprise Bean Client Using Greedy Enumeration

Session bean client

Another example of a finder executed in greedy mode is when a session bean with its transaction attribute set to TX_NOT_SUPPORTED calls findAll(), as shown in Figure 67.

```
// Client code
...
MySessionBean s = ...
s.m1();

// Session EJB code
void m1() {
   ...
   Enumeration result = entityHome.findAll();
   // lazy finder being enumerated within the same transaction
   while (result.hasMoreElements()) {
      Object o = result.nextElement();
      ...
   }
   ...
}
```

Figure 67. Session Bean Using Greedy Enumeration

In Figure 68, the finder will execute in **lazy** mode, since there is a transaction active at the time the finder was invoked. The enumeration will work as expected, since it is being exhausted within the same transaction used to invoke the finder.

```
...
UserTransaction utx = ...
utx.begin();
Enumeration result = entityHome.findAll();
// enumerating result in same transaction as used to invoke the finder
while (result.hasMoreElements()) {
   Object o = result.nextElement();
   ...
}
utx.commit();
...
```

Figure 68. Client using lazy enumeration from within its originating transaction

Pure Java enterprise bean client programming errors
In Figure 69, the finder executes in **lazy** mode since there is a transaction active at the time it is invoked. The call to `result.nextElement()` will fail with an `IllegalStateException`, because the transaction used to invoke the finder has committed.

```
...
UserTransaction utx = ...
utx.begin();
Enumeration result = entityHome.findAll();
utx.commit();
// can't enumerate result after committing the transaction
while (result.hasMoreElements()) {
   Object o = result.nextElement();
   ...
}
...
```

Figure 69. Client using lazy enumeration outside its originating transaction

Session enterprise bean

In Figure 70, a session bean (TX_REQUIRED) invokes an entity bean finder. The finder will execute in **lazy** mode since there is a transaction active at the time the finder is invoked. So we enumerate the result within the same transaction.

```
// Client code
...
MySessionBean s = ...
s.m1();

// Session EJB code
void m1() {
   ...
   Enumeration result = entityHome.findAll();
   // lazy finder being enumerated within the same transaction
   while (result.hasMoreElements()) {
   Object o = result.nextElement();
   ...
   }
...
}
```

Figure 70. SB returning a Lazy Enumeration after Enumerating it

Session enterprise bean programming errors

In Figure 71, a session bean (TX_REQUIRED) invokes an entity bean finder. The finder executes in **lazy** mode since there is a transaction active at the time the finder is invoked. The session bean attempts to return the Enumeration to the client. The Enumeration will fail with an IllegalStateException on the client, because the transaction in which the finder was invoked has committed. (The transaction in this case was the transaction started by the container when m1() was invoked.)

```
// Client code
...
MySessionBean s = ...
Enumeration result = s.m1();
while (result.hasMoreElements()) {
    Object o = result.nextElement();
    ...
}

// Session bean code
Enumeration m1() {
    ...
    Enumeration result = entityHome.findAll();
    // Enumeration will become invalid once m1 returns
    return result;
}
```

Figure 71. SB Returning a lazy Enumeration; Client Tries to Enumerate it

Back to Session enterprise bean correctly programmed
The example in Figure 72 shows how you can use a session bean to invoke an entity bean finder and return results to the client successfully. The Enumeration is walked within the transaction and the results are stored in a non-volatile Vector.

```
// Client code
...
MySessionBean s = ...
Vector result = s.m1();

// Session bean code
Vector m1() {
    ...
    Vector result = new Vector();
    Enumeration e = entityHome.findAll();
    // lazy finder being enumerated within same transaction
    while (e.hasMoreElements()) {
        result.addElement(e.nextElement());
    }
    return result;
}
```

Figure 72. SB Returning a Copy of an Enumerated Lazy Enumeration

In Figure 73, a session bean (TX_REQUIRED) invokes an entity bean finder. The finder executes in **lazy** mode since there is a transaction active at the time the finder is invoked. This shows that the session bean can return the enumeration to the client if the client started the transaction.

```
// Client code
...
MySessionBean s = ...
UserTransaction utx = ...
utx.begin();
Enumeration result = s.m1();
// result enumerated in same transaction as finder executed
while (result.hasMoreElements()) {
   Object o = result.nextElement();
   ...
}
utx.commit();

// Session bean code
Enumeration m1() {
 ...
 Enumeration result = entityHome.findAll();
 return result;
}
```

Figure 73. SB returning a lazy enumeration; client controls the transaction

8.2.4 Enumerations test scenarios

For this redbook, we developed a simple example that features the elements described above. We added some tracing mechanism to be able to capture the exact behavior of the IBM WebSphere Advanced Edition run-time when dealing with enumerations.

This simple application has one container managed persistent bean: Customer. On the CustomerHome, we have defined a findAll() method that retrieves all the customer instances.

The client application invokes findAll() in both greedy and lazy mode. The database table for customer is initialized with 100 records.

Given this configuration, we could observe the behavior described in the following scenarios.

8.2.4.1 Finder executed in greedy mode

In this scenario, the client does not start a transaction (see Figure 74) before calling findAll() method.

```
public void findAllGreedy() {
Enumeration listOfCustomers=null;
Customer customer=null;
try {

    listOfCustomers = CustomerHome.findAll();
    System.out.println("findAll executed successfully ");
    while(listOfCustomers.hasMoreElements()) {
        customer = (Customer)
        PortableRemoteObject.narrow(listOfCustomers.nextElement(),
        Customer.class);
        System.out.println("Greedy: from Java client without transaction
        demarcation, customer name is : " + customer.getName());
    }
}catch (FinderException e) {System.out.println("findAll failure " +
e);}
catch (RemoteException e) {System.out.println("findAll failure " + e);}
catch (Exception e) {System.out.println("Exception on findAll " + e);}

}//end method
```

Figure 74. Client Code for Greedy Mode

As the client iterates through the enumeration, we can see the server behavior, as shown in the following trace (see Figure 75).

```
instance id= 0  ----->  ejbActivate
instance id= 0  ---------->  ejbLoad
instance id= 0  ------------  getName:  Joaquin 0
instance id= 0  <----------  ejbStore
instance id= 0  <-----  ejbPassivate
instance id= 1 ----->  ejbActivate
instance id= 1  ---------->  ejbLoad
instance id= 1  ------------  getName:  Joaquin 1
instance id= 1  <----------  ejbStore
instance id= 1  <-----  ejbPassivate
...
instance id= 98 ----->  ejbActivate
instance id= 98  ---------->  ejbLoad
instance id= 98  ------------  getName:  Joaquin 98
instance id= 98  <----------  ejbStore
instance id= 98  <-----  ejbPassivate
```

Figure 75. Server Side While the Client Iterates Through the Enumeration

For each call to getName, the server instantiates the corresponding bean which goes through a complete life cycle:

- ejbActivate
- ejbLoad
- getName
- ejbStore
- ejbPassivate

This is repeated on the server side for each element until the last one.

8.2.4.2 Pool size impact on greedy enumeration

In IBM WebSphere Advanced Edition, the container has a parameter (Cache Size) that can be set to a given value. This value specifies how many instances the container maintains in its pool.

Given this information, we may wonder what happens when the number of elements goes beyond the cache size? In this case, we may expect an exception to be thrown to the client.

When the client invokes findAll(), it receives the exception:

```
java.rmi.NoSuchObjectException: CORBA INV_OBJREF 0 No; nested exception is:
org.omg.CORBA.INV_OBJREF:   minor code: 0  completed: No
```

8.2.4.3 Finder executed in lazy mode

In this scenario, the client starts a transaction, calls findAll(), and iterates through the enumeration as shown in Figure 76.

```
public void findAllLazy() {
Enumeration listOfCustomers=null;
Customer customer=null;
try {
    javax.transaction.UserTransaction utx = (javax.transaction.UserTransaction)
    ic.lookup("jta/usertransaction");
    utx.begin();
    listOfCustomers = customerHome.findAll();
    System.out.println("findAll executed successfully ");
    while(listOfCustomers.hasMoreElements()) {
        customer = (Customer)
        PortableRemoteObject.narrow(listOfCustomers.nextElement(),
        Customer.class);
        System.out.println("Lazy: from Java client WITH transaction
        demarcation,customer name is : " + customer.getName());
    }
    utx.commit();
}catch (FinderException e) {System.out.println("findAll failure " + e);}
catch (RemoteException e) {System.out.println("findAll failure " + e);}
catch (NamingException e) {System.out.println("utx failed " + e);}
catch (Exception e) {
    System.out.println("utx failed " + e);
    System.out.println("printStack ");
    e.printStackTrace();
}
}//end method
```

Figure 76. Client Code for Lazy Mode

On the server side, we can observe that the server picks a chunk of five instances from the pool and calls ejbl oad (see Figure 77, top) before invoking the business method, getName() in our example.

As the client iterates through the collection, the server keeps loading instances until the last element of the enumeration is requested. They remain loaded until the transaction is committed.

When the client commits the transaction, the server starts a cycle of calls to ejbStore on all instances still active, and then ejbPassivate (see Figure 77, bottom). The call to ejbStore may appear slightly strange, since the server does not need to store anything. This can be avoided by declaring in VisualAge for Java the getName method as **Const Method**. In that case, ejbStore is not called.

```
instance id= 0  ---------->  ejbLoad
instance id= 1  ---------->  ejbLoad
instance id= 2  ---------->  ejbLoad
instance id= 3  ---------->  ejbLoad
instance id= 4  ---------->  ejbLoad
instance id= 0  ------------  getName:  Joaquin 0
instance id= 1  ------------  getName:  Joaquin 1
instance id= 2  ------------  getName:  Joaquin 2
instance id= 3  ------------  getName:  Joaquin 3
instance id= 4  ------------  getName:  Joaquin 4
...
instance id= 95  ---------->  ejbLoad
instance id= 96  ---------->  ejbLoad
instance id= 97  ---------->  ejbLoad
instance id= 98  ---------->  ejbLoad
instance id= 99  ---------->  ejbLoad
instance id= 95  ------------  getName:  Joaquin 95
instance id= 96  ------------  getName:  Joaquin 96
instance id= 97  ------------  getName:  Joaquin 97
instance id= 98  ------------  getName:  Joaquin 98
instance id= 99  ------------  getName:  Joaquin 99
......
......
instance id= 77  <----------  ejbStore
instance id= 76  <----------  ejbStore
instance id= 75  <----------  ejbStore
...
instance id= 1  <----------  ejbStore
instance id= 0  <----------  ejbStore
instance id= 99  <----------  ejbStore
instance id= 98  <----------  ejbStore
...
instance id= 78  <----------  ejbStore
instance id= 77  <-----  ejbPassivate
instance id= 76  <-----  ejbPassivate
...
instance id= 1  <-----  ejbPassivate
instance id= 0  <-----  ejbPassivate
instance id= 99  <-----  ejbPassivate
...
instance id= 79  <-----  ejbPassivate
instance id= 78  <-----  ejbPassivate
```

Figure 77. Server trace for loading and unloading of collections

8.2.4.4 Pool size impact on lazy enumeration

We have already talked about the container cache size parameter in 8.2.4.2, "Pool size impact on greedy enumeration" on page 110 for greedy enumeration. Now let us see its influence on lazy enumerations.

Unlike for greedy enumeration, the client calls findAll, which is successfully executed. Then it starts iterating through the enumeration. The server loads chunks of five elements until it reaches the maximum available in the pool. In this situation, a timeout is started and if no instance has been freed before the timer expires then the transaction is rolled back and the exception is thrown to the client:

```
com.ibm.ejs.persitence.EnumeratorException original exception:
javax.transaction.TransactionRolledbackException
```

You may ask, which strategy you should adopt in this case? You may increase the cache size, but it will not guarantee that the problem will not occur again with a larger enumeration.

8.2.5 Summary

8.2.5.1 Lazy behavior

A home finder method invoked in an existing transaction, results in the activation of the first five elements. As the client walks through the returned enumeration, the server activates the next five elements until the last element of the enumeration is reached. Activated beans can be used as long as the transaction in which the finder was invoked has not yet committed.

8.2.5.2 Greedy behavior

In contrast, a home finder method invoked without an existing transaction returns a greedy enumeration. A client can iterate through the entire enumeration and if no business method is invoked, the server does not activate a bean.

Only an enterprise bean's remote interface methods invocation (for example getName()) starts an activation cycle:

- ejbActivate,
- ejbLoad,
- business method invocation (example: getLastname())
- ejbStore,
- ejbPassivate.

This activation cycle is repeated for each method invoked on a bean.

8.3 Using the JDBC API

We have seen how we can handle collections by using finders. For
performance reasons, it may be acceptable to use direct JDBC programming
instead

In this case, we have a more powerful way of getting and manipulating a
collection of records. Let us see what we get by using the JDBC API.

8.3.1 ResultSet

The result of executing an SQL Select statement with JDBC is a ResultSet.
The client program can extract the column values of the rows retrieved by
iterating through the rows of the ResultSet. In JDBC 1.0, only forward
scrolling through a ResultSet is supported. JDBC 2.0 adds backward scrolling
and update capability for the ResultSet.

8.3.1.1 ResultSet types
The supported result types are:

- Forward-only (JDBC 1.0 forward-only result type)
- Scroll-insensitive (static view of the contents)
- Scroll-sensitive (dynamic view of the contents)

Scrolling is the ability to move forward (first-to-last) and backward
(last-to-first) through the contents of the result set.

Result set types which support scrolling allow a particular row to be visited
multiple times while a result set is open. So the ability to make changes in the
underlying data visible to the application, which we call sensitivity, is definitely
relevant.

8.3.1.2 Scrolling and concurrency
The supported concurrency types are:

- Read-only: This increases the level of concurrency as read-only locks are
  not limited in numbers on the database
- Update: This reduces concurrency as only one write lock may be held at a
  time.

When concurrency occurs, it is clear that all of the updates that a transaction
makes are visible to itself, whereas the changes (updates, inserts, and
deletes) made by other transactions may or may not be visible to a particular
transaction. If updates made by one transaction are visible to another

transaction then the changes will be visible through the result set opened in this other transaction.

Visibility through a result set means that depending on its result set type, while it is open, it may or may not expose changes to its underlying data made by other transactions or other result sets that are part of the same transaction. This feature is determined by the transaction isolation level.

8.3.1.3 Performance
You can specify, at the result set level:

- The number of rows to be fetched when more rows are needed
- The direction for processing the rows (forward, reverse, or unknown).

In the end you have the option of writing an application using an optimistic concurrency control scheme if data access conflicts are rare.

8.3.2 Transaction isolation level

The transaction isolation level, since JDBC 1.0, determines whether changes made by other transactions are visible to the current transaction.

```
/**
    * Dirty reads, non-repeatable reads and phantom reads can occur.
    */
int TRANSACTION_READ_UNCOMMITTED = 1;

/**
    * Dirty reads are prevented; non-repeatable reads and phantom
    * reads can occur.
    */
int TRANSACTION_READ_COMMITTED   = 2;

/**
    * Dirty reads and non-repeatable reads are prevented; phantom
    * reads can occur.
    */
int TRANSACTION_REPEATABLE_READ  = 4;

/**
    * Dirty reads, non-repeatable reads and phantom reads are prevented.
    */
int TRANSACTION_SERIALIZABLE     = 8;
```

The isolation level for a given transaction can be set by calling the setTransactionIsolation method on a Connection:

```
con.setTransactionIsolation(TRANSACTION_READ_COMMITTED);
```

If all transactions in a system execute at the TRANSACTION_READ_COMMITTED isolation level or higher, then a transaction will only see the committed changes of other transactions.

8.3.3 Coding examples

In this section we show a few examples of JDBC coding and scrolling of result sets.

Forward-only and read-only result set (JDBC 1.0 like)

No transaction isolation level is specified, so a default value is taken.

```
Connection con = DriverManager.getConnection("jdbc:db2:SAMPLE");
Statement stmt = con.createStatement();
ResultSet rs = stmt.executeQuery("SELECT emp_no, salary FROM employee");
```

Forward-only and sensitive result set

Rows of data are requested to be fetched twenty-five at-a-time.

```
Connection con = DriverManager.getConnection("jdbc:db2:SAMPLE");
Statement stmt = con.createStatement(ResultSet.TYPE_SCROLL_SENSITIVE,
ResultSet.CONCUR_UPDATABLE);
stmt.setFetchSize(25);
ResultSet rs = stmt.executeQuery("SELECT emp_no, salary FROM employee");
```

A prepared statement can be used as well.

```
PreparedStatement pstmt = con.prepareStatement(
"SELECT emp_no, salary FROM employees where emp_no = ?",
ResultSet.TYPE_SCROLL_SENSITIVE,
ResultSet.CONCUR_UPDATABLE);
pstmt.setFetchSize(25);
pstmt.setString(1, "060366");
ResultSet rs = pstmt.executeQuery();
```

Update

The application can update, insert, delete rows in an updateable result set. It has to position within the result set and then update, insert or delete.

An update example is (columns may be specified by name or number):

```
rs.first();
rs.updateString(1, "100");
rs.updateFloat("salary", 100000.0f);
rs.updateRow();
```

An insert example is:

```
rs.moveToInsertRow();
rs.updateString(1, "101");
rs.updateFloat(2, 200000.0f);
rs.insertRow();
//leave insert row and return to the row that was the current row before
rs.first();
```

Cursor movements

Examples of iteration are:

- Full forward iteration:

```
rs.beforeFirst();
while (rs.next()) {
    System.out.println(rs.getString("emp_no") + " " +
                        rs.getFloat("salary"));
}
```

- Full backward iteration:

```
rs.afterLast();
while (rs.previous()) {
    System.out.println(rs.getString("emp_no") + " "+
                        rs.getFloat("salary"));
}
```

8.3.4 Caveats

It is up to the application developer to check the actual result set type used:

```
aResultSet.getType();
aResultSet.getConcurrency();
```

As a matter of fact, the result set type asked for may not be supported by the JDBC driver you use (in which case you will probably get an SQL warning), or it may not even be possible for the kind of statement you have issued.

For example a SELECT statement that contains a join over multiple tables may not end up into an updatable result set.

However:

- It should be updatable queries on a single table, with no join operations, and selecting the primary key.
- It should be insertable queries that select all non-nullable columns and all columns that don't have a default value.

Visibility of updates have the following characteristics:

- A result set can or can not see its own changes (inserts, updates, and deletes). This capability varies between DBMSs and JDBC drivers.
- A scroll-insensitive result set, once it is opened, does not make any visible changes that are made by other transactions or other result sets in the same transaction. It can be seen as a private copy of the result set's data.

  A scroll-sensitive result set makes all of the updates visible, made by others that are visible to its enclosing transaction. Column values are always visible. However, inserts and deletes may not be visible.

8.3.5 RowSet

"Just a nice extension of ResultSet": a JavaBean using a datasource.

The interest of a Rowset is that it is a JavaBean that encapsulates a set of rows, without necessarily maintaining an open database connection. If necessary, an optimistic concurrency control mechanism is used.

8.3.6 Using JDBC with a stateless session bean

To come back to our main purpose which is about collections, we can use direct JDBC code encapsulated in a session bean. The session bean provides a service that can return a vector containing all the attribute values corresponding to a given query for display purpose.

Once the user has selected a record then the corresponding enterprise bean can be used in combination with other enterprise beans involved in the same unit of work.

8.4 Conclusion

You need to understand lazy and greedy enumerations before using finders.

With lazy enumerations, you have to keep in mind that invoking a finder on the server side involves the activation of five instances. As the client iterates through the enumeration the server activates the next chunk of five elements. If the number of elements goes beyond the number of instances available in the pool then the server throws an exception and rolls back the transaction.

With greedy enumerations, each call to a business method results in a complete activation cycle. If the number of elements in the enumeration resulting from the execution of the finder is greater than the number of available instances in the pool, the finder returns an exception.

During our tests, we did some measurements to compare the different approaches. Iterating through a greedy is twice as fast as a lazy enumeration if only one method is invoked on each instance.

However, as the number of methods invoked on an instance increases, the lazy enumeration provides better performances.

If you really need speed, you can skip bean activation by using JDBC.

For example, assume we want to display on a browser customer ID and name for a hundred of customers. From this list, the user can select one customer and request details.

An implementation that calls a home finder to retrieve these two customer's attributes results in the activation of each instance, including hydrating all object's attributes. This represents a useless system overhead.

Instead, we prefer to delegate the creation of the list to JDBC, and only when details are requested, we use the findByPrimaryKey finder on the home to activate the corresponding bean.

Then we get full benefit of using enterprise beans by combining this and other bean instances in a single unit of work.

Part 2. Design patterns and guidelines

In the first part of this redbook, the reader was given guidelines about the technology choices and architecture for Web applications.

This second part of the book is structured like the book "Design Patterns: Elements of Reusable Object Oriented Software" (see B.3, "Other resources" on page 184).

The user who is only interested in a given problem can go directly to the discussion of design considerations and possible solutions for the given problem.

Chapter 9. Servlets/JSP pattern and guidelines

In this chapter we provide specific guidelines on how to organize an application using servlets and JSPs.

9.1 Servlet/JSP pattern

With this pattern it is possible to organize a Web application into servlets and JavaServer Pages in such a way that it is easy to maintain the code.

9.1.1 Motivation

For applications that require complex modeling on the Web application server node, it is not easy to define the granularity of servlets and how servlets interact. But without a good design for the servlets and JSP it is hard to maintain the application.

In addition in the analysis phase of a project, use cases and state transition diagrams are widely used to describe the result of the analysis phase. It would be helpful to map those results in the design and implementation phase.

One extreme design approach is to have only one servlet per use case. The servlet then acts as the central event handler and processes all requests from the client. It executes the necessary action for that event and forwards the request to one (of many) JavaServer Page for displaying the result. By using this solution, it may be difficult to develop that servlet. As it is responsible for a whole use case, we may have to implement a lot of logic in that servlet.

The other extreme is to have as many servlets as JavaServer Pages and to "chain" them. This means that a servlet gets a request, executes the proper action, and calls the JavaServer Page specific to that servlet to display the result. A request from that JSP then gets to another servlet and so on. This approach will be hard to maintain since having many servlets and JSP can get confusing when trying to figure out the flow of the application.

We provide a solution that has a granularity between those extreme approaches by dividing the application in different states. We try to transfer a state transition diagram (for example, modeled with RationalRose) into HTML pages, servlets and JavaServer Pages.

9.1.2 Applicability

This pattern can be used in all servlet /JSP applications. We recommend this pattern especially in complex Web applications where many Web pages and page transitions have to be developed.

9.1.3 Structure

The structure of the Servlet/JSP pattern is shown in Figure 78.

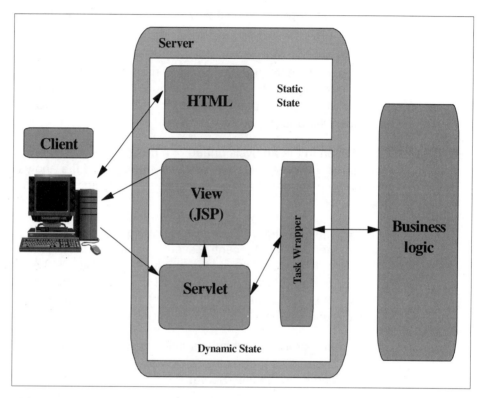

Figure 78. Structure of the Servlet/JSP pattern

9.1.4 Participants

The participants in this structure are:

- **Servlet**: A given request either gathers data needed for the display of a given state or invokes the action causing a transition out of the state. This responsibility makes it the "controller" in a Model-View-Controller (MVC) based application.

- **JavaServer Pages**: Handles the generation of HTML code for a given request result.

- **Task wrapper**: Encapsulates access to the enterprise business process (back-end data and function). This function makes the Task Wrapper the "model" in a MVC application.

- **HTML page**: In case of static content and state transitions, we do not need complex technologies. An HTML page handles the "static" states.

9.1.5 Collaborations

A Web application flow can be captured in a state transition diagram (which is, by the way, a good documentation for the application flow). A state transition diagram contains named states which are connected with named branches.

For our solution, we map each component of the state transition diagram to a component of our e-business architecture that can be managed by the WebSphere Application Server.

We separate the states in the diagram into static states, and dynamic states. State transitions from static states are inherent. As they are static in content and in transitions, we can code one state as one HTML page which should be named after the state: <State>.html.

When it comes to the dynamic states, life is a bit more difficult. Conforming to our e-business architecture, we divide the state into model, view and controller.

Controller

The servlet acts as the controller for one state in our scenario. This means that we get one servlet per dynamic state. By naming convention, the servlet is named after the state: `<State>Servlet`. By doing this we get an easy method of documentation.

We think about each interaction between the browser and the Web application server (for example, the servlet) as a single unit of work, either read-only or update. There are two basic flows of control patterns, both implemented by the servlet. One handles the display for a given state, and the other handles the actions that cause a state change.

Display pattern

This pattern is usually manifested within HTML as a link, resulting in a GET request. The flow of control for this pattern is:

1. The servlet invokes the appropriate read-only method on the model of the state (that is the task wrapper, see below) and selects the JavaServer Page to handle the result.

2. The servlet initializes the data object associated with the JavaServer Page, loads it with the result and sets the view bean into an HttpRequest attribute.

3. The servlet forwards the request to the chosen JavaServer Page.

4. The JavaServer Page generates the HTML code.

Update pattern

This pattern is usually manifested within HTML as a form action of some sort, resulting in a POST request. The flow of control pattern is likewise simple, but since it represents a transition to some next state, actually employs the Display pattern to handle processing of the next state.

1. The servlet determines the type of action to be taken (usually from the submit button value), and selects the appropriate update method on the model (which is the Task Wrapper, see below).

2. The servlet accesses the input parameter for the Task Wrapper method from the request object and invokes the method.

3. Based on the result, the servlet does a state transition using the `sendRedirect()` method to the "next" state.

4. This causes the display pattern for the next state to be invoked.

A data object is a JavaBean with simple `getXXX()` and `setXXX()` methods which encapsulates a bulk of data. For more information about data objects, see 10.2, "EJB session facade to entity beans" on page 157.

View

The view is implemented as a JavaServer Page. Here, we use the same naming convention. This means that a JavaServer Page is named after its state: <State>.jsp. If you have more than one JavaServer Page associated with one state (for example, a separate error page) we recommend that you start the name of every JavaServer Page belonging to one state with the name of that state, for example <State>Error.jsp.

Model

We define a *task wrapper* class which is responsible to group the methods of the given task that are likely to be implemented in a similar fashion into a single object.

The task wrapper encapsulates the access to the enterprise business process (that is, back-end data and function). This function makes the task wrapper the "model" in the MVC pattern. As we want to get many parameters to and from the task wrapper, we use data objects for each method when the result is more than a single value.

State transitions

An interesting point is how to design and implement the state transitions. A straightforward solution is to forward to the next state within a servlet, when an update has to be done (as mentioned in the Update Pattern section). If we need a state transition by pressing the "submit" button on the screen, we can let the JavaServer Page or HTML page point directly to the new state (which means to the servlet of that state). This approach is quite simple, but it is difficult to maintain such an application, because state transitions are handled in servlets and JavaServer Pages.

A more consistent approach would allow state transitions only from servlets. This means that a JavaServer Page always calls the servlet belonging to the same state. That servlet would execute the state transition by redirecting to the new state servlet. We need to be aware that we have to keep track of the servlets internal state, as it may be called several times. This can be done by storing the state in the session object or by integrating it into the active JavaServer Page.

9.1.6 Consequence

By using this pattern, we get a good approach for designing a Web application.

9.1.7 Implementation

The implementation of the task wrapper and the servlet is detailed here.

9.1.7.1 Task wrapper

The task wrapper could be implemented as a stateless session bean. This means that it runs on the EJB server and, therefore, it executes local calls when accessing the EJB.

It is a good idea to encapsulate that session bean with a Java class, so that it is easier for the servlet programmer to access the session bean. Therefore, we need a Java class with the same methods as in the session bean. If we use a class with static methods for accessing the session bean, it is easy to cache the InitialContext and rarely changing read-only data within one JVM, so that we get a performance benefit.

If we have the following attributes in this static class:

```
private static InitialContext nameContext = null;
private static ThisTaskSessionHome taskSessionHome = null;
private static ThisTaskSession taskSession = null;
```

We can use:

```
private static TasksSession getTasksSession() {
   try {
      if (nameContext == null) {
         Properties p = new Properties();
         p.put(
         javax.naming.Context.INITIAL_CONTEXT_FACTORY,
         "com.ibm.ejs.ns.jndi.CNInitialContextFactory"
         );
         nameContext = new InitialContext(p);
      }
      if (tasksHome == null) {
         Object homeObject = nameContext.lookup("ThisTasksSession");
         tasksHome = (ThisTasksSessionHome)
                     javax.rmi.PortableRemoteObject.narrow(
                         homeObject, ThisTasksSessionHome.class);
      }
      if (tasksSession == null) {
         tasksSession = tasksHome.create();
      }
      return tasksSession;
   }
   catch (Exception e) {
      return null;
   }
}
```

To implement a task wrapper method like:

```
public static synchronized void denyRequest (String serialNumber)
{
   try {
      getTasksSession().denyRequest (serialNumber);
   } catch (Exception e) {
   }
}
```

9.1.7.2 Servlet

The implementation of the servlets is straightforward to the patterns given above. Because we do not implement anything else in the servlets, they become very mechanical. The implementation of the display pattern, for example, could be:

```
public void doGet (HttpServletRequest req, HttpServletResponse res)
             throws ServletException, IOException
{
    // This will handle read and display from the Manager screen
    String serialNumber = req.getParameter("serialNumber");
    req.setAttribute("ManagerCheckInView",
    Tasks.getManagerCheckInView(serialNumber));

    getServletContext().getRequestDispatcher
            ("/Application/ManagerCheckIn.jsp").forward(req,res);
}
```

It is an interesting idea to create a superclass for the servlets when we discover similarities in their behavior. For example if we require that a user has to be logged on for our application, this check could be done in the superclass. The proper action, for example, display a logon JavaServer Page, could be included in that servlet.

9.1.8 Related pattern

The servlet/JSP pattern makes use of the following patterns:

Data object: Data objects are used as a contract in the input and output parameter of a task wrapper and between the servlet and JavaServer Page.

Command: The task wrapper of our pattern is somehow equivalent to a command bean. But while the task wrapper typically has multiple methods, each representing a unit of work associated with the underlying business process, there is one command bean for each unit of work. This means that a difference is the granularity they address.

Facade: It is the responsibility of the task wrapper to execute the right business logic. This is a good point to integrate the facade pattern, so that the task wrapper uses the facade to call the business logic.

9.2 XML data islands

In this section we describe the XML data island pattern.

To include a view of an XML stream in our application, we introduce *XML data islands*. The XML data island is a generic JavaBean that takes XML data, then formats it using a given XSL stylesheet, and returns a piece of HTML code which can be included in a JavaServer Page.

9.2.1 Motivation

In our programming model we use servlets and JavaServer Pages to display information to the client, because this is an easy and straightforward way.

But in many cases we have to deal with XML as XML becomes more and more popular, especially as an exchange language between software components. It is often required to display those XML data. Therefore, we can use XSL (eXtensible Stylesheet Language) to format a given XML document into HTML. But it would be convenient to integrate XML and XSL into our JavaServer Page or servlet driven architecture. As WebSphere has a built-in XSL Processor (Lotus XSL) for converting an XML document into an HTML page, there should be a way to use that XSL processor within a JavaServer Page.

9.2.2 Applicability

Use this pattern when you want to integrate XML data with an XSL stylesheet in a JavaServer Page.

9.2.3 Structure

The structure of the XML data island pattern is shown in Figure 79.

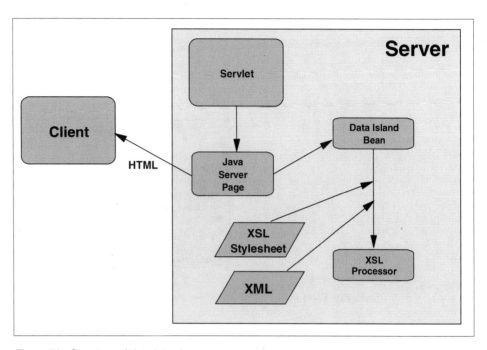

Figure 79. Structure of data island

9.2.4 Participants

The **JavaServer Page** acts as the view in our application. It is responsible for the output page to the user. The JavaServer Page is the "host" for the XML data island and includes the resulting HTML code.

The **XML data island Bean** is used to integrate the XML data and the XSL stylesheet into the JavaServer Page. Its detailed structure is seen in Figure 80. The URLs of the XML data and the XSL stylesheet have to be set using the setXml() and setXsl() methods. Then the getDocument() method can be called to get the HTML code.

The **XSL Processor**, which is included in WebSphere, is used to convert the XML data into HTML code using a given XSL stylesheet.

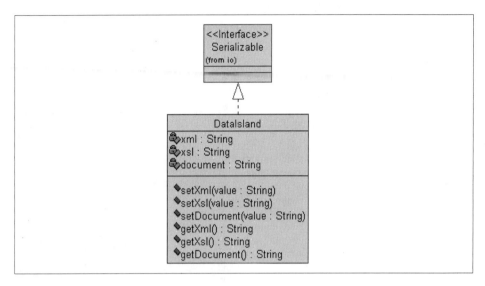

Figure 80. Class model of the XML data island

9.2.5 Collaboration

The XML data island is created by the JavaServer Page. By calling the getDocument() method, the data island creates an instance of the XSL processor, passes the URL for both XML data and XSL stylesheet to the processor and invokes it. The result, the HTML code, is stored in the **document** property and returned to the JavaServer Page. There the HTML code is included.

9.2.6 Consequence

With XML data islands we get the opportunity to include XML data in our Web pages. We get a complete and integrated architecture.

9.2.7 Implementation

The implementation of the bean, JSP< and XML is detailed here.

The XML data island bean
It is the XML data island's responsibility to call the XSL processor with the XML document and the XSL stylesheet. Therefore, we must import the XSL processor classes.

We declare the class, which simply extends *Object*:

```
package itso.dg.xml;
```

```
import java.lang.*;
import java.util.*;
import com.ibm.xml.parser.*;
import com.lotus.xsl.*;
import java.io.*;

public class DataIslandBean implements java.io.Serializable
{
   // Attributes
   protected String xml = "";
   protected String xsl = "";
   protected String document = "";

   // Define Methods here
}
```

The HTML code and the URLs for the XML document and the XSL stylesheet
are stored in a bean property. Therefore, we must provide get and set
methods for them:

```
public String getXml () { return xml; }

public void setXml (String value) { xml = value; }

public String getXsl (String value) { return xsl; }

public void setXsl (String value) { xsl = value; }

public void setDocument (value) { document = value; }
```

The real work is done by the get method of the document property. It gets the
URL for the XML data and the URL of the XSL stylesheet and calls the XSL
Processor to transform the XML data, using the instructions in the XSL
stylesheet. The resulting data is stored in the document property:

```
public String getDocument () {
   try {
      ByteArrayOutputStream stream = new ByteArrayOutputStream ();
      PrintWriter pw = new PrintWriter (stream);
      XSLProcessor processor = new XSLProcessor ();
      processor.process (xml, xsl, pw);
      document = stream.toString ();
   } catch (Exception e) {
      document = "Error in XSL processing: " + e.getMessage ();
   }
   return document;
}
```

The "host" JavaServer Page which includes the XML data island

The JavaServer Page has to add a useBean tag, to set the URLs for the XML document and the XSL stylesheet and to call the getDocument() method where appropriate:

```
<%@ page import = "itso.dg.xml.DataIslandBean" %>
<jsp:useBean id="dataIslandBean" class="itso.dg.xml.DataIslandBean"
            scope="session"/>
<jsp:setProperty name="dataIslandBean" property="xml" value="XML-URL"/>
<jsp:setProperty name="dataIslandBean" property="xsl" value="XSL-URL"/>
<%= dataIslandBean.getDocument() %>
```

XML data input

Because we are passing only the URL to the XML document, it could be in a file as seen in the example below. But it does not need to be on the Web server.

The XML document could be constructed by another servlet. If the URL of this servlet is set to the XML data island Bean by the JavaServer Page, its output would be converted to HTML.

9.2.8 Sample code

For this example, we use the XML file seen in Figure 81 and the XSL stylesheet seen in Figure 82. For the example, both files have to be in the /xml directory of the Web server.

```
<?xml version = "1.0"?>
<spec>
   <title>Configuration for ACME Mega Server </title>
   <model>AMS 9000</model>
   <parts>
      <part>
         <number>9000</number>
         <description>Mode 9000</description>
         <list-price>$2,000.00</list-price>
      </part>
   </parts>
   <list-subtotal>$2,000.00</list-subtotal>
</spec>
```

Figure 81. XML data island code: specs.xml

```
<?xml version="1.0"?>
<xsl:stylesheet xmlns:xsl="http://www.w3.org/1999/XSL/Transform"
version="1.0">
<xsl:template match="/">
    <H1> <xsl:value-of select="spec/title"/> </H1>
    <P> <xsl:value-of select="spec/model"/> </P>
    <TABLE BORDER="1">
       <TR>
          <TH>Part#: </TH>
          <TH><xsl:value-of select="spec/model"/></TH>
          <TH>List Price</TH>
       </TR>
       <xsl:for-each select="spec/parts/part">
       <TR>
          <TH><xsl:value-of select="number"/></TH>
          <TH><xsl:value-of select="description"/></TH>
          <TH><xsl:value-of select="list-price"/></TH>
       </TR>
       </xsl:for-each>
    </TABLE>
</xsl:template>
</xsl:stylesheet>
```

Figure 82. XML data island code: specs.xsl

JavaServer Page

Using the data island Bean is easy. We need to add a bean tag into the
JavaServer Page and then call the getDocument() method where we want the
data bean to be displayed:

```
<%@ page import = "itso.dg.xml.DataIslandBean" %>
<jsp:useBean id="dataIslandBean" class="itso.dg.xml.DataIslandBean"
            scope="session"/>
<jsp:setProperty name="dataIslandBean" property="xml"
                value="http://localhost:8080/spec/spec.xml"/>
<jsp:setProperty name="dataIslandBean" property="xsl"
                value="http://localhost:8080/spec/spec.xsl"/>
<HTML>
   <HEAD> <TITLE>XML data island Sample</TITLE> </HEAD>
   <BODY>
      <H2> data island Example</H2>
      <P>
         <%= dataIslandBean.getDocument() %>
      </P>
   </BODY>
</HTML>
```

9.2.9 Related patterns

It is possible to integrate the **command pattern** and the XML data island pattern. This results into a display command which calls some commands with XML results. The display command then converts the XML data into HTML code using the technique of the data island.

A similar approach is described in the redbook *Enterprise JavaBeans Development Using VisualAge for Java*, SG24-5429. They introduce **XSLT islands**, which are scriptlets embedded in a JavaServer Page. The scriptlets contain the XSL code directly. They use the Bean Scripting Framework (BSF) available on alphaWorks to integrate JSP, XML and XSL.

9.3 Applet to server communication

Building applets is a powerful way of extending HTML pages with dynamic and sophisticated interfaces. Sun's Java Application Programming Model recommends using HTML, JavaServer Pages and also applets on the client. In many cases we just have to implement some presentation logic in the applets. Sometimes the applet has to put or get information from the server during runtime.

An easy and straightforward way for the communication from an applet to a server uses Java's built-in mechanism for remote communication, RMI. Although this idea seems simple, we can run into problems with this approach.

First, using RMI means that we open our application to the Internet by offering a RMI server to the world which is usually not desired. Firewalls, which are used to secure the server and clients, will usually block incoming traffic on all ports, only the port used by HTTP gets through, so that RMI communication will fail.

Second, in our e-business architecture we propose the use of servlets as the connection point to the client. Since the standard way of talking with servlets is based on HTTP, we cannot use RMI.

9.3.1 Applet to servlet communication using HTTP

Since the HTTP port is usually the only communication port from the applet to the servlet, we need a way to connect to the server via HTTP which makes it easy to use servlets.

The strategy is to write servlets and let them run in on the server. The servlets are called by applet wrapping the communication in HTTP requests.

Java provides an API for that kind of communication. To open an HTTP connection, we have to use the URL and the URLConnection classes which make it easy to read and write data from a URL. All we have to do is to make an URL connection to the servlet, write the output text to the HTTP stream and read the incoming text.

The following code snippet shows this part of an applet:

```
private String callServlet (String city) {
String input = "";

try {
   URL url = new URL
   ("http://localhost/servlet/AppletCommServlet");
   URLConnection connection = url.openConnection ();
   connection.setUseCaches (false);
   connection.setDoOutput (true);

   OutputStream out = connection.getOutputStream();
   PrintWriter print = new PrintWriter (out);
   print.println ("city=" + city);
   // print.write (city);
   print.flush();
   print.close();

   InputStream in = connection.getInputStream ();
   DataInputStream textStream = new DataInputStream (in);

   input = textStream.readLine ();
   in.close();
} catch (Exception e) {
   buffer.append ("Exception: " + e);
   System.out.println ("Exception: " + e);
}
return input;
}
```

On the server-side we need just a regular servlet. Since the HTTP issues are handled by WebSphere we have to implement the proper action. The service() method could be:

```
public void service (HttpServletRequest request,
      HttpServletResponse response) throws java.io.IOException {
   String city;
   PrintWriter writer = response.getWriter();

   city = request.getParameter ("city");
```

```
    // do something
    System.out.println ("city: " + city);

    // answer to applet
    writer.println ("95123");  // zip code of city
}
```

One advantage of carrying text over the network is the compatibility with existing servlets, because the applet may use the same format as HTML forms. But on the other hand it is arduous coding and decoding text streams. Fortunately, HTTP connections can also carry binary data. This allows us to transport whole Java objects (this is called firewall tunneling) using the content-type:

```
application/x-www-form-urlencoded
```

We flatten the objects we want to carry into a binary stream and use HTTP to convey the binary data. On the other side we de-flatten the stream back into objects and use them.

The object flattening can be done by the standard object serialization built in Java. An object can be serialized if its class implements the java.io.Serializable interface. The default implementation of the serialization is sufficient in most cases. Therefore, there is no need to code anything for serialization. If we require special treatment during serialization and deserialization, we must implement the following two methods:

```
private void writeObject (java.io.ObjectOutputStream out)
            throws IOException;
private void readObject (java.io.ObjectInputStream in)
            throws IOException, ClassNotFoundException;
```

Then we wrap the OutputStream from the URLConnection in an ObjectOutputStream and write the serialized object on the stream. The same applies to the input stream, we must wrap it into an ObjectIntoStream.

As we have to deal with object streams only, the code is nearly the same on the applet and on the servlet. Therefore, we show the applet code only:

```
private UserInfo callServlet () {
String input = "";

try {
    URL url = new URL ("http://localhost/servlet/AppletCommServlet1");
    URLConnection connection = url.openConnection ();
    connection.setUseCaches (false);
```

```
                    connection.setDoOutput (true);
                    connection.setRequestProperty ("content-type",
                                    "application/x-www-form-urlencoded");

                    OutputStream out = connection.getOutputStream();
                    ObjectOutputStream objectOutStream = new ObjectOutputStream (out);
                    objectOutStream.writeObject (new UserInfo());

                    InputStream in = connection.getInputStream ();
                    ObjectInputStream objectInStream = new ObjectInputStream (in);

                    UserInfo i = (UserInfo)objectInStream.readObject();
                    in.close();
            } catch (Exception e) {
                buffer.append ("Exception: " + e);
                System.out.println ("Exception: " + e);
            }

            return i;
            }
```

Using object serialization and the standard HTTP protocol is a simple way for an applet to communicate with a servlet. Because it does not require an open socket (like RMI), it is scalable. You have to be aware that serialization is a feature of the JDK 1.1 and it won't work with old browsers.

9.3.2 Applet to server-object communication using IIOP

Sometimes it makes sense to access backend objects like EJB directly from the applet. RMI-IIOP is emerging as the standard protocol to access enterprise beans on the server. Here are the issues:

- EJB containers communicate via IIOP or RMI over IIOP. This causes problems using firewalls described above.

- Since not all browser support RMI over IIOP, we are limited in the browser we support.

- Applets are, by default, limited to communicate only with the server that they originate from, therefore, the EJBs will have to be there. We can get around this with certificates, but this complicates the design and the administration.

- EJB are not easy to access from applets or from pervasive clients without any Java support.

Therefore, the standard solution is to develop a servlet / JSP front end with a HTML interface. Despite this option, in many cases it is required to develop application or applet-based clients that can access EJBs across the Internet.

Since the Internet firewalls let the HTTP protocol pass, we need to have a protocol on top of HTTP which allows remote object calls. At the moment there is no standard definition of such a protocol, but many ideas are forth coming.

It could be an option to encapsulate one or more EJB interaction from the client into an XML message. This XML document can be shipped over HTTP to a servlet which reads the document and calls the EJB by reflection. The result can be shipped to the client as an XML stream again.

XML seems perfect for this solution since it allows not only Java clients to connect to the beans. Even a lightweight JavaScript client could use the EJB. With XML we are not restricted to HTTP either. This offers us the chance to access EJB objects and methods across all kinds of protocols like MQSeries.

There are two approaches:

- A very complex but powerful approach uses its own definition language. Like in RMI or CORBA, you will need to define an interface and pre-compile the objects to define stubs and skeletons.

- A more dynamic way is the one described above. Here we don't need any fixed information as the reflection-api is used to call the methods.

9.4 Pushing[1] content to the client

When developing an e-business architecture we have many interactions between the client and the server. The characteristics of most e-business applications show that communication happens only if the client (that is, the browser) initiates an event.

Sometimes it is necessary to update the client's data from the server without having a client requesting the information. This is what we call *push technology.* A typical application using push technology would be a flight information system on the Internet with automated arrival, departure and delay time display.

Push technology makes it possible for the server to update content on the client as it changes rather than having the client go to look for it.

[1] Based on Just van den Broecke's article http://www.javaworld.com/javaworld/jw-03-2000/jw-03-pushlet.html

The next few sections offer solutions for pushing content to the client.

9.4.1 Automatic reload of HTML page

An easy way of updating information on the client is not to push the information to the client but to have the client automatically reload the HTML content of the page.

If we use the "Refresh" meta tag in an HTML page:

```
<META HTTP-EQUIV="Refresh" CONTENT="2;URL=http://bismuth/servlet/MyServlet">
```

Every two seconds, the browser will reload the page with the URL:

```
http://bismuth/servlet/MyServlet
```

This line of code can of course not only be included in static HTML pages but also in JavaServer Pages and servlets. The following example shows a servlet which is reloaded every two seconds:

```
public class ReloadServlet extends HttpServlet
            implements java.io.Serializable {
public void service (HttpServletRequest request,
      HttpServletResponse response) throws java.io.IOException {
  HttpSession session;
  Writer out;
  int i = 1;
  Date date = new Date ();

  out = response.getWriter ();
  response.setContentType ("text/html");

  out.write ("<html><head><title>Yet another test</title>");
  out.write ("<META HTTP-EQUIV=\"Refresh\"
    CONTENT=\"2;URL=http://bismuth/servlet/ReloadServlet\"> ");
  out.write ("</head><body><H1>Test1:" + date + "</H1></body></html>");
  out.flush();
}
}
```

This solution is very simple and is useful only in special situations. Since the refresh time of the HTML page is fixed and independent of the change of the content you can't be sure that the client has the up-to-date information. On the other hand, if the content changes rarely, the refresh may happen without having updated content. Therefore, this solution needs more resources (that is, servlet invocations) than necessary.

9.4.2 Applets

Another, more sophisticated solution uses applets on the client. The applet is able to connect to the server using RMI or CORBA and passes a remote reference of a client object to the server as a callback. The server notifies the client by calling the remote object on the client which can display the new content in a Java GUI (using AWT or Swing).

Using applets with RMI/CORBA is an object-oriented way of pushing data to the client and displays it the way you need. The server does not have to worry about the technology as this solution is completely based on Java. The server knows that the pushed data has been processed by the client and will get an exception in case of a failure.

A big problem with the applet communication using RMI or CORBA is that it does not use the standard HTTP port and protocol to communicate. Therefore, the used ports may not be opened by a firewall and this technology will fail. Another point worth mentioning is that we are using a different technology on the client than HTML. This has consequences on the application development (since the presentation programmer has to have Java knowledge) and on the client technology. The browser must support Java and RMI/CORBA. Problems may occur when a different version of the JDK is used on the client and on the server because of different RMI implementations.

Using RMI/CORBA callback is convenient when used in an intranet environment, because you don't have to worry about bandwidth (that is, the applet will be loaded fast) and about firewalls. In an intranet environment you can have full control over the browser (and plugins) installed on the clients with system management tools like Tivoli so that you can avoid problems with different JDK versions.

9.4.3 Open socket communication

Another approach avoiding the problems with the firewall uses a push technology with just HTML (DHTML preferred) on the client and a normal servlet on the server-side. To keep up the communication between client and server, *HTTP streaming* is used. This technology is often seen on multimedia Web sites where realtime audio or video data is transferred to the client, and this simply means that the socket will not be closed after surrendering the HTML code.

The approach is easy. In the servlet we are not closing the HTTP connection (by returning from the doGet() / doPost() method). Instead we are pushing data to client whenever we need it. The following code shows an example which appends a new line every two seconds:

```
public void service (HttpServletRequest request,
    HttpServletResponse response) throws java.io.IOException {
    Writer out;
    int i = 1;

    out = response.getWriter ();
    response.setContentType ("text/html");

    while (i++ < 20) {
        out.write ("<H1>" + new Date() + "</H1>");
        out.flush();
        try {
            Thread.sleep (2000);
        } catch (InterruptedException e) {
            out.write (e.toString());
        }
    }
}
```

Usually we don't want to append information to the existing, but replace it. This is a bit more tricky, because we have to use at least JavaScript and the browser's document object model (DOM).

The idea is to write a callback function in JavaScript which is embedded into the HTML page (generated by the servlet/JSP). Since we have an open socket connection we can call this function when needed by pushing a call to the function to update the information on the client. Now we have two choices:

The content we want to update is embedded in a browser element, such as an input field. Then the following servlet snippet shows a possible solution (the HTML code embedded in the servlet should go into a JSP, of course):

```
public void service (HttpServletRequest request,
    HttpServletResponse response) throws java.io.IOException {
    HttpSession session;
    Writer out;
    int i = 1;

    out = response.getWriter ();
    response.setContentType ("text/html");
    // output javascript function
    out.write ("<html>");
    out.write ("<head>");
```

```
out.write ("<title> JavaScriptPushServlet </title>");
out.write ("<script language=\"JavaScript\">");
out.write ("function changeContent (c)");
out.write ("{document.form.text.value=c}");
out.write ("</script>");
out.write ("</head>");
out.write ("<body>");
out.write ("<form name=\"form\">");
out.write ("<input type=\"text\" name=\"text\" value=\"\" size=25>");
out.write ("</form>");
out.write ("Test");
out.write ("</body>");

while (i++ < 20) {
    out.write ("<script language=\"JavaScript\"> changeContent(\"" +
               new Date() + "\")</script>");
    out.flush();
    try {
       Thread.sleep (2000);
    } catch (InterruptedException e) {
       out.write (e.toString());
    }
  }
}
```

If we need to update a bigger section like a frame (or the whole page), it is more complicated. We have to use frames and dynamic HTML (DHTML). DHTML gives us the possibility to access and to change all documents in the browser with the DOM. We need a main page which defines a frameset with two frames. One will be a visible page (with a dummy content in the beginning) and the other one will be an invisible frame pointing to our servlet (see Figure 83).

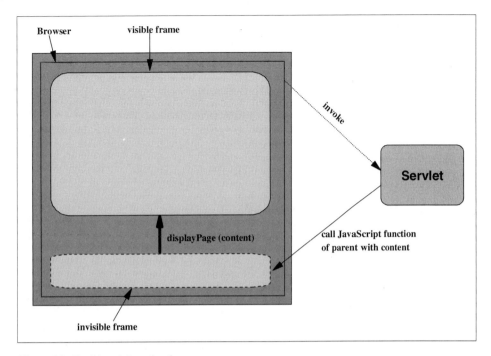

Figure 83. Pushing data using frames

The main page also defines the callback JavaScript function which gets a new HTML page from the servlet and displays it in the first frame:

```
<HTML>
<HEAD>
<META http-equiv="Content-Type" content="text/html; charset=iso-8859-1">
<META HTTP-EQUIV="Pragma" CONTENT="no-cache">
<script LANGUAGE="JavaScript">
    function displayPage(content) {
        window.frames['page'].document.writeln(content);
        window.frames['page'].document.close();
    }
</script>
</HEAD>

<FRAMESET BORDER=0 COLS="*,0">
    <!-- display -->
    <FRAME SRC="pushframe.html" NAME="page" BORDER=0 SCROLLING=no>
    <!-- Hidden -->
    <FRAME SRC="/servlet/PushServlet" NAME="dummy" BORDER=0 SCROLLING=no>
</FRAMESET>
</HTML>
```

Where `pushframe.html` is a dummy page, displayed until the servlet outputs its first page:

```
<HTML> <BODY> </BODY> </HTML>
```

The PushServlet's service method creates the new HTML pages and invokes the callback method in the frame:

```
public void service (HttpServletRequest request,
     HttpServletResponse response) throws java.io.IOException {
   HttpSession session;
   Writer out;
   String content;

   out = response.getWriter ();
   response.setContentType ("text/html");
   // response.setHeader ("pragma", "no-cache");

   out.write ("<BODY>");
   try {
      while (true) {
         try {
            Thread.sleep(3000);
         } catch (InterruptedException e) {
            out.write (e.toString());
         }
         content = "<HTML><BODY>";
         content += "<H1>The current time is: " + new Date() + "</H1>";
         content += "</BODY></HTML>";
         out.write ("<script language=JavaScript >parent.displayPage ('" +
         content + "')</script>");
         out.flush();
      }
   } catch (Exception e) {
   out.write (e.toString());
   }
   out.write ("</BODY>");
}
```

This approach integrates perfectly in our e-business scenario using only HTML and JavaScript on the client and servlets on the server. Since we are using pure HTTP firewall the problems described for the RMI/CORBA callback solution do not occur. In addition we don't have to get additional code to the browser. That reduces not only the loading time, but also the resource consumption on the browser and the requirements to the browser.

On the other hand, we demand DHTML on the browser when displaying new HTML pages. Most browsers fulfill this requirement, but some old browsers will not display the content.

9.4.4 Consequences of using push technology

It is tempting to use push technology. There are many fields where we want the user to be up to date, and push technology seems to be a good solution. But you have to be careful implementing a push server. The big problem about push technology (except for the first approach using the refresh, which isn't a real push technology) is the scalability. In an e-business application there may be hundreds of clients connected to the application. For each client we need an open socket. As a consequence these clients are tied to a specific machine.

Another problem of push technology is, when using the open HTTP connection, the server does not get an acknowledge of the data coming in by the client.

When implementing a push technology we have often one data source in our system which feeds the client. In the flight information system sample we would have a component with the flight information and many clients accessing the data via push technology. Therefore, it can be useful to design a system as seen in Figure 84, with the observer pattern (see GAMMA) where the data source is the subject of the information and the servlets connected to a client observe the data source.

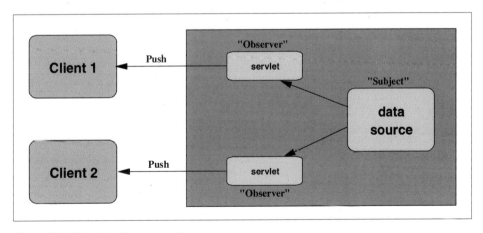

Figure 84. Using the Observer pattern

Chapter 10. EJB design patterns

In this chapter we provide specific guidelines on how to facilitate access to EJBs using design patterns.

10.1 Factory for EJB Homes

The home factory pattern provides the following benefits:

- Insulate EJB clients from Naming Service complexity.
- Cache naming context creation and EJB home lookup for getting better performance.
- Provide an interface for creating EJB homes without specifying the method to use to narrow to the concrete class at run-time.

This pattern is also known as Home Factory or Home Caching.

10.1.1 Motivation

Before invoking an EJB's business method, a client must create or find an EJB object for that bean. To create or find an instance of a bean's EJB object, the client must:

1. Locate and create an EJB home object for that bean.
2. Use the EJB home object to create or find an instance of the bean's EJB object.

JNDI is used to find the EJB home object by name. Here are the properties that an EJB client uses to initialize JNDI and find an EJB home that are stored in a resource bundle. See 10.1.7, "Implementation" on page 153 for further details.

To initialize a JNDI name service, an EJB client must set the appropriate values for the following JNDI properties:

- `javax.naming.Context.PROVIDER_URL`: This property specifies the host name and port of the name server used by the EJB client, in the format `iiop://hostname:port`.
- `javax.naming.Context.INITIAL_CONTEXT_FACTORY`: This property identifies the actual name service that the EJB client must use (in WSAE, this property must be set to `com.ibm.ejs.ns.jndi.CNInitialContextFactory`).

Locating an EJB home object is a two-step process:

1. Create a javax.naming.InitialContext object.
2. Use the InitialContext object to create the EJB home object.

Creating an InitialContext object involves the following code:

```
// Get the initial context
if (initContext == null) {
   try {
      Properties properties = new Properties();
      // Get location of name service
      properties.put(javax.naming.Context.PROVIDER_URL,
                   bundle.getString("providerUrl"));
      // Get name of initial context factory
      properties.put(javax.naming.Context.INITIAL_CONTEXT_FACTORY,
                   bundle.getString("nameService"));
      initContext = new InitialContext(properties);
   } catch (Exception e) { // Error getting the initial context
      ...
   }
}
```

Here we construct a java.util.Properties object, add values to the Properties object, and then pass the object as the argument to the InitialContext constructor. The resource bundle class may be instantiated by calling the ResourceBundle.getBundle method. The values of variables within the resource bundle class are extracted by calling the getString method on the bundle object.

After the InitialContext object is created once, it remains good for the life of the client session, provided it is stored appropriately as a class or instance attribute. Therefore, the code required to create the InitialContext object is placed within an if statement that determines if the reference to the InitialContext object is null. If the reference is null, the InitialContext object is created; otherwise, the reference can be reused on subsequent creations of the EJB object.

Getting the EJB home object involves the following code:

```
// Look up the home interface using the JNDI name
try {
   java.lang.Object homeObject =
           initContext.lookup(bundle.getString("myHomeName"));
   myHome = (MyHome)javax.rmi.PortableRemoteObject.narrow(
              (org.omg.CORBA.Object) homeObject, MyHome.class);
} catch (Exception e)  { // Error getting the home interface
   ...
}
```

After the InitialContext object (initContext) is created, the application uses it to create the EJB home object by invoking the lookup method, which takes the JNDI name of the enterprise bean in String form and returns a java.lang.Object object.

After an object is returned by the lookup method, the static method javax.rmi.PortableRemoteObject.narrow is used to obtain an EJB home object for the specified enterprise bean. The narrow method takes two parameters: the object to be narrowed and the class of the EJB home object to be returned by the narrow method. The object returned by the javax.rmi.PortableRemoteObject.narrow method is cast to the class associated with the home interface.

- As we have seen, getting access to EJB homes is complex (initial context, home lookup, home narrow).
- Very simple caching can be implemented for the naming context, but still needs a more clear design.
- Home lookup caching is required because lookup operation involves at least inter-process communication (between application server and admin server), and possibly network round trip (for clients obtaining their initial context from a remote machine), hence a negative impact on performance.
- Finally, the environments in which you are testing and/or deploying may require a different narrow method, in which case this has to be encapsulated and made transparent into a factory-like service.

10.1.2 Applicability

Use the home factory pattern when:

- The result of EJB homes lookups should be cached for performance reasons.
- A client should be configurable to access different sets of classes, implementing an EJB with the same EJB home JNDI name.
- The client should be independent of how the EJB homes are narrowed.

The first bullet has proven to be a mandatory requirement in any real-life application.

10.1.3 Structure

The structure of the home factory pattern is shown in Figure 85.

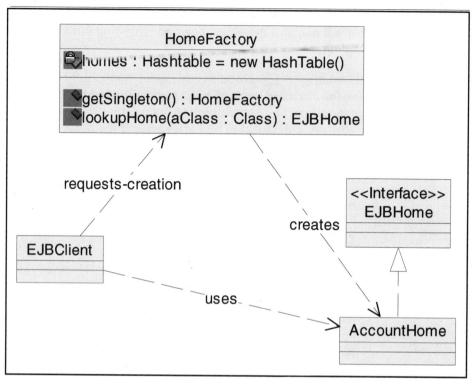

Figure 85. HomeFactory Class Diagram

10.1.4 Participants

The participants in the home factory pattern are:

- HomeFactory

  - Declares and implements an interface for:
    - The operation that returns the factory singleton
    - The operation that returns the EJB homes

- EJBClient

  - Uses interface declared by HomeFactory

10.1.5 Collaborations

There is not much collaboration because the HomeFactory is the only class:

- A single instance of Homefactory is created at run-time. This HomeFactory creates EJB homes as defined in an externalized manner, for example, by means of resource bundles or XML files.

- HomeFactory uses the metadata stored in this externalized manner for instantiating and returning the appropriate EJB home class.

10.1.6 Consequences

The home factory pattern has the following benefits:

1. *It promotes consistency among clients*: When naming context and EJB homes are accessed in the same way, it is easy to modify and/or enhance the level of service provided by the factory.

2. *The support of new kinds of EJB homes is transparent*: If specified externally, EJB homes and their concrete classes can be added and made available without effort.

3. *It isolates the EJB home actual classes*: The factory encapsulates and as such isolates clients from actual EJB home concrete classes, as far as those concrete classes are not needed for usage (that is, none of their specific methods are called).

10.1.7 Implementation

1. *Factory as singleton*: This ensures that only one instance of the factory class is created, and that this one instance is accessible to all clients; all clients get access to this instance by calling the class's getSingleton static method, rather than by constructing the instance by themselves; so the class's constructors are private (be sure to declare at least one private constructor; otherwise, a default public constructor will be automatically generated).

Factory as singleton

```
public class HomeFactory {
    private static HomeFactory singleton = null;
    ...
private HomeFactory() {
    super();
    }
    ...
public static HomeFactory getSingleton() {
    if (singleton == null) {
            singleton = new HomeFactory();
    }
    return singleton;
}
    ...
}
```

2. *Loading externalized information*: the properties that an EJB client uses to initialize JNDI and find an EJB home object may vary across EJB server implementations. To make an enterprise bean more portable between EJB server implementations, we have to externalize these properties in environment variables, XML files, properties files, or resource bundles, rather than hard code them into the EJB client code. The first issue we face is the EJB home fully qualified class name to be used for narrowing the result of the lookup. Here we give an outline of reading XML files.

Loading externalized information

```
public class HomeFactory {
   ...
   private static ConfigurationData configuration = null;
   ...
public static ConfigurationData getConfigurationData() {
   if (aConfigurationData != null) {
      return aConfigurationData;
   }
   ConfigurationData aConfigurationData = new ConfigurationData();
   ...
   // obtaining an input stream and a DOM parser
   ...
   Document document = parser.readStream(inputStream);
   ...
   NodeList nodeList = document.getElementsByTagName("entity-bean");
   int length = nodeList.getLength();
   for (int i = 0; i < length; i++) {
      EnterpriseBeanMetaData
      enterpriseBeanMetaData = new EnterpriseBeanMetaData();
      enterpriseBeanMetaData.readElement((Element) nodeList.item(i));
      Class homeClass = enterpriseBeanMetaData.getHomeClass();
      ConfigurationData.setEnterpriseBeanMetaData(homeClass,
            enterpriseBeanMetaData);
   }
   ...
   configuration = aConfigurationData;
   return aConfigurationData;
}
...
}
```

3. *Specifying externalized information*: XML formatting for EJBHome, EJB remote interface, EJB class, EJB primary key class (if applicable), JNDI name, naming context implementation class name and provider URL; alternatives are environment properties, resource bundle, properties file.

```
┌─ Information in XML format ──────────────────────────────────────┐
 <configuration>
 <jndi-property>java.naming.factory.initial=com.ibm.ejs.ns.jndi.CNInit
 ialContextFactory
 </jndi-property>

 <jndi-property>java.naming.provider.url=iiop://127.0.0.1:900
 </jndi-property>
 <enterprise-beans>
    <entity>
       <jndi-name>AccountHome</jndi-name>
       <home>itso.dg.ejb.AccountHome</home>
       <helper-class>javax.rmi.PortableRemoteObject</helper-class>
    </entity>
 </enterprise-beans>
 </configuration>
```

4. *Caching initial context and EJB homes*: the initial context is a single object, whereas, EJB homes are cached in a hash table with the JNDI names as keys; the point is that we can take benefit of the meta-information stored in the XML file specifying the EJB implementation classes for writing a full generic version of the `lookupHome` method.

Naming context and EJB homes caching

```java
public class HomeFactory {
...
private Hashtable homes = new Hashtable();
...
public static EJBHome lookupHome(Class aClass)
    throws RemoteException {
try {
   EJBHome home = (EJBHome) homeCache.get(aClass);
   if (home != null) {
      return home;
   }
   ConfigurationData aConfigurationData = getConfigurationData();

   EnterpriseBeanMetaData enterpriseBeanMetaData =
      aConfigurationData.getEnterpriseBeanMetaData(aClass);

   InitialContext initialContext = new
      InitialContext(enterpriseBeanMetaData.getJndiProperties());

   String lookupString = enterpriseBeanMetaData.getJndiHomeName();
   Object anObject = initialContext.lookup(lookupString);

   Method narrowMethod = enterpriseBeanMetaData.getNarrowMethod();
   if (narrowMethod == null) {
      home = (EJBHome) anObject;
   } else {
      Object[] parameters = new Object[] {anObject, aClass};
      home = (EJBHome) narrowMethod.invoke(null, parameters);
   }
   if (home == null) {
      return null;
   }
   homeCache.put(aClass, home);
   return home;
} catch (Exception ex) {
   ex.printStackTrace();
   return null;
}
}
}
```

5. *Concurrency*: Multiple client threads may use the factory at the same time; we assume that it is better to let clients engage in looking up the same EJB home concurrently, and then update the same entry multiple times in the hash table (with the same value, as expected), rather than serializing access to a method or a resource other than the hash table synchronized put method.

10.1.8 Known uses

This work was based on the Freeside demo application (WebSphere Application Server sample application) and on the home factory developed for the ITSO banking application (see *Enterprise JavaBeans Development Using VisualAge for Java*, SG24-5429).

10.1.9 Related patterns

The *singleton pattern* is a well known design pattern.

10.2 EJB session facade to entity beans

A facade provides a unified interface to a set of interfaces in a subsystem (see Gamma, E. et al., Design Patterns: Elements of Reusable Object Oriented Software).

In the EJB world the EJB session facade pattern provides a stable, high-level gateway to the server-side components. An EJB session facade hides the entity bean interfaces to the clients.

10.2.1 Motivation

An entity bean represents an object view of a business entity stored in persistent storage and includes business logic to manipulate the bean state. In addition an entity bean implements business logic dealing with entity specific business rules. For example, the account bean implementation checks the overdraft before allowing a withdraw. Entity beans are fine-grained components.

In contrast, business processes often involve multiple entity beans. For example, the business process (use case) 'transfer an amount from Account A to Account B' involves a withdraw on AccountA and a deposit on AccountB. Furthermore, the transfer use case should run within a unit of work.

We do not recommend that a client interacts directly with entity beans, because it ties the client directly to the details of the business entities. Any changes in the interface of the entity beans and their interactions require changes to the clients, and it is very difficult to reuse the code that models the workflow.

Session beans are better suited to deal with multiple-entity business logic. Session beans are coarse-grained components that allow clients to perform tasks without being concerned with the details that make up the task. This allows developers to update the session bean internals, with the possibility to change the workflow, without impacting the client code.

An EJB session facade to entity beans has another benefit: performance improvement. Accessing coarse-grained session beans from the client instead of fine-grained entity beans reduces the number of remote method invocations.

10.2.2 Participants

The participants in this pattern are:

- EJB session facade
- Entity bean

10.2.3 Implementation

When implementing the facade pattern we have to decide the structure of the facade class, the granularity of facade objects, and structuring and abstracting the input and output parameters.

Stateless versus stateful session beans
The choice of the EJB session type (stateless or stateful) depends on several factors:

- Use case type

  - Non-conversational: This is where the entire use-case is completed with a single session method invocation.

  - Conversational: Requires more than a single session method invocation by a particular client with state maintained between invocations.

- Client type

  - Web client (servlet invoked via Web browser and HTTP protocol)
  - Java application (via RMI/IIOP protocol)

- Scalability

- Performance

- System resources

- Availability

We suggest that you implement non-conversational use cases with stateless session beans. Stateless session beans are scalable and, in comparison to stateful session beans, need less system resources and perform better.

We implement client neutral conversational use cases with stateful session beans. The homes of stateful sessions are scalable; stateful session beans themselves are not. The homes allow stateful session beans to be created on a group of servers (clones), each with client affinity to the one it happened to be created on. This means that stateful session beans are likely to be spread over all the clones in a workload managed environment which gives a measure of load balance. Each method invocation goes to the server who created the bean. The bean may be gone if the server has crashed, but this is the expected behavior. The EJB specification states that session beans do not survive server crashes. A Web client (servlet) can store the handle of a session bean in the HTTPSession object.

For a Web-centric (Web client only) application we could consider maintaining the conversational state in a HTTPSession instead of a stateful session bean. The WebSphere session clustering mechanism serializes the Java objects stored in the HTTPSession in a database. This approach enables a scalable and fault-tolerant solution. In this scenario we would implement the session facade as stateless session bean.

For developing a fault-tolerant, client independent conversational use case we consider implementing the conversational state with an entity bean behind a stateless session facade. This pattern is out of the scope of this redbook.

Custom finders for update transactions
In session facade methods, entity beans are typically activated and loaded by their homes. The method gets the primary key fields of the entities via parameters. To prevent database deadlocks in update transactions we recommend that you define and implement custom finders which lock the rows at load time (SQL SELECT FOR UPDATE). For a detailed discussion see 11.1.3, "Database deadlocks" on page 174.

Isolation level dependencies
Within a transaction context the isolation level associated with the first method invocation becomes the required isolation level for all methods invoked within that transaction. If a method is invoked with a different isolation level than that of the first method, the IsolationChangeException is thrown.

In an EJB session facade pattern the invoked session method typically, implicitly, or explicitly starts (and commits or rolls back) a transaction. The isolation level attribute of the invoked session methods therefore determines the isolation level for the transaction context.

Entity method invocations via copy helper access beans

An EJB session facade collaborates with fine-grained entity beans. The usage of copy helper access beans can help to decrease the number of remote method invocations.

For a detailed discussion see 6.2, "Copy helpers" on page 56.

Granularity

Facades are built by the business logic programmer. The requirements are usually coming from the use case analysis and define calls to the business logic. Each of those coherent calls is implemented as a separate facade method.

An interesting aspect is the size of a facade object. One extreme would be to define one facade class per invocation. As we get a lot of facade classes, we do not recommend this. The other extreme leads us to one big facade class with all interface methods to the business logic included for an application. This may be a good approach in a small application, but in a bigger application the facade object is getting very large. The right approach will be usually in the middle of both extremes. One possibility is to collect the calls for one subsystem (such as a shopping subsystem or a CRM subsystem) in one facade class.

Data objects

Facades will provide a high-level interface to the inside of the components. This has consequences on input and output parameters of the facade methods. That means that a facade never returns a reference to an EJB object, because the EJB technology is hidden behind the facade. Instead we may return only a key to an EJB object. The input and output parameters of a facade method are coarse grained. A good way of defining and implementing those parameters is by using data objects.

A data object is a local only object with simple `getXXX()` and `setXXX()` methods. An extreme approach makes a data object "immutable" with read-only properties and a special constructor that takes all of the properties in one shot. This approach reinforces the notion that it is a contract object between two components and prevents the facade client from inadvertently updating the data. A data object is serialized so that it can be passed by value to and from EJB based implementations for the facade.

In our approach we recommend to use the data objects to return results, if the return value is more than a single primitive type. We are a little more flexible when it comes to the input parameters. If the method has more than one, we do not prescribe that there must be a data object, although these can be very handy.

Since data objects are coded as JavaBeans, it is a good idea to use them directly in a JavaServer Page. That means that the servlet acts as a facade's client and therefore executes the business logic by calling the facade methods. The returned data object is directly passed to the JavaServer Page, where its data can be displayed.

Since data objects transfer data only, an alternative could be XML. Therefore, we must define DTDs for the input and the output parameters of the facade methods. The signature of all methods would have a string as input parameter and as the return type. This approach has the advantage that we are more flexible in defining the contract between the client and the facade. But on the other hand we have to interpret the incoming and outgoing XML stream, both in the facade and in the client of the facade. This could be a performance problem.

10.2.4 Related patterns

The EJB facade pattern is related to the command pattern.

Command pattern: If we are developing an e-business architecture with many EJBs, it is useful to encapsulate them with the facade pattern. This solves the problem of the complexity of our business logic but we still have a performance problem. If the servlet invokes the facade objects directly, we can get multiple round-trips because different facade objects may be invoked. This is a good application for the command pattern: The servlet calls the command which is transferred to the server. There it performs method calls to the facade. The result, the data object, is stored in the command bean and transferred back to the client (see Figure 86).

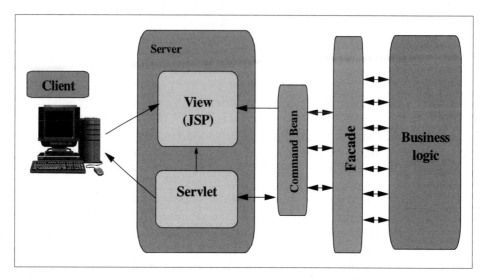

Figure 86. Collaboration between command pattern and facade pattern

10.3 Optimistic locking pattern

The optimistic locking pattern ensures entity integrity with short lock cycles. This approach reduces overall locking overhead and improves total system throughput and performance.

10.3.1 Motivation

Obviously we expect optimistic locking support as part of the application server infrastructure (transparent container service). The aim of this section is to provide an application pattern for runtimes without optimistic locking infrastructure support.

IBM WebSphere Enterprise Edition / Component Broker 3.02.1 provides support for optimistic locking through its caching service by mouse-click. Such an optimistic locking support for entities is neither part of the EJB specifications nor IBM WebSphere Advanced Edition 3.02.1.

A user request may result in starting a transaction which should also be terminated before returning an answer to the user. As a general rule, transactions (and associated locks) should not span user think-time.

We discuss this issue with the proposed locking mechanism approach based on the following use case.

A user needs to update the customer information. For that purpose, he goes through these steps:

- Get a copy of customer data (first transaction)

- Modify this copy

- Send the copy to the server side to make this update permanent (second transaction)

It could happen that another user concurrently accesses the same data for update as described in this scenario:

1. userA requests a copy of customerA's data

2. userB requests a copy of customerA's data

3. userA changes customerA's name from 'Kurt Weiss' to 'Martin Weiss'

4. userB changes customerA's birthdate from 57/05/01 to 55/08/08

5. userA sends the changed copy for server-side update

6. userB sends the changed copy for server-side update

How can we prevent the updates made by userB from overriding those of userA?

The answer resides in the implementation of an update service. This additional service is in charge of checking that the persistent customer data has not been modified since a copy was sent to the user.

10.3.2 Applicability

The optimistic locking pattern applies to:

- IBM WebSphere Advanced Edition

- Commit option C (of the EJB specifications)

10.3.3 Participants

The participants in the optimistic locking pattern are:

- EJB session facade

    - Generic, unified copy / update service for entities

- EJB entity home

    findByPrimaryKey (for copy services)

    - Custom finder (for update services)

- EJB entity bean
  - Accessed concurrently from different transactions
  - Timestamp field
- EJB entity bean copy
  - Serializable copy of the bean state
- Database manager
  - Responsible for managing concurrency with commit option C
  - Timestamp setting via insert and update triggers

10.3.4 Implementation

This section describes the optimistic locking pattern for IBM WebSphere Advanced Edition. The pattern is based on an optimistic lock service implemented as a stateless session bean. The optimistic lock service is a generic, unified session facade for copying and updating all optimistic lockable entities.

10.3.4.1 Optimistic lockable entity bean

The optimistic lockable entity bean has the following characteristics:

- The remote interface extends from OptimisticLockable (see Figure 87). The entity bean implements the copy and update methods.

```
public interface OptimisticLockable {
   public OptimisticLockableEntityCopy copy() throws
      java.rmi.RemoteException;
   public void update(OptimisticLockableEntityCopy entityCopy) throws
      java.rmi.RemoteException;
}
```

Figure 87. OptimisticLockable interface

- A java.sql.Timestamp field (lastModified) in the implementation of the bean. The timestamp represents the creation time or the last update of the bean's state.

  As the timestamp is a usual persistent field, it has to be part of the underlying database table.

Database triggers are responsible for setting the timestamp. For each of the underlying database tables, we define two triggers: a before_insert trigger and a before_update trigger. See Figure 93 on page 170 for a concrete example.

This approach makes the scalability of the application easier. Delegating the timestamp setting to the bean implementation would rely on synchronized clocks (application server clones). The approach with the database triggers is application server independent.

We do not implement a getter and setter for the timestamp field in the bean.

- For the update service: a custom finder in the entity's home implementing a read-for-update (with an SQL clause "FOR UPDATE"). The parameter list includes:
  - Primary key field(s) of the bean
  - Timestamp

For the copy service we use the findByPrimaryKey finder method of the bean's home.

10.3.4.2 Copy class for each optimistic lockable entity

For each optimistic lockable entity, a copy class must be implemented. This copy class extends from OptimisticLockableEntityCopy (see Figure 88).

The OptimisticLockableEntityCopy base class has lastModified as a protected member. Each concrete copy class has to implement the three methods:

- findEntity
- findEntItyForUpdate
- getHomeName

The getHome method of base class delegates the naming service (home lookup, and narrows the remote reference to the appropriate type) to the Home Factory. For a detailed discussion see 10.1, "Factory for EJB Homes" on page 149.

```
public abstract class OptimisticLockableEntityCopy
                  implements java.io.Serializable {
  public abstract javax.ejb.EJBObject findEntity() throws
      javax.ejb.FinderException, java.rmi.RemoteException;
  public abstract javax.ejb.EJBObject findEntityForUpdate() throws
      javax.ejb.FinderException, java.rmi.RemoteException;
  protected abstract String getHomeName();
  public OptimisticLockableEntityCopy(java.sql.Timestamp
                              argLastModifier) {
      lastModified = argLastModified;
  }
  public java.sql.Timestamp getLastModified() {
      return lastModified;
  }
  protected java.sql.Timestamp lastModified;
}
protected javax.ejb.EJBHome getHome() throws java.rmi.RemoteException {
    String homeName = getHomeName();
    //HomeFactory class is an implementation of the Factory for EJB Homes
    //pattern published in the redbook 'Servlet/JSP/EJB Design
    //and Implementation Guide for IBM WebSphere Application Servers'.
    //HomeFactory narrows the remote reference to the appropriate type.
    javax.ejb.EJBHome home =
        itso.dg.ejb.base.HomeFactory.getSingleton().lookupHome(homeName);
    if (home == null)
        throw new java.rmi.RemoteException("home with name '" + homeName
                    + "' not found or narrowing error");
    else
        return home;
}
```

Figure 88. OptimisticLockableEntityCopy class

The optimistic lock service (session facade for copying and updating all optimistic lockable entities) has two methods:

- Copy entity
- Update entity

For both methods we set the transaction attribute to TX_REQUIRES_NEW. With this transaction settings we enforce both methods to run in an own transaction context with a short commit cycle and lock time, respectively.

In Figure 89 we show the implementation of the copyEntity method.

```
public OptimisticLockableEntityCopy copyEntity
   (OptimisticLockableEntityCopy copyWithEntitySearchArgs)
   throws javax.ejb.FinderException, java.rmi.RemoteException {
   //find entity (read-only)
   EJBObject ejbObject = copyWithEntitySearchArgs.findEntity();
   if (ejbObject instanceof OptimisticLockable) {
      return ((OptimisticLockable)
         javax.rmi.PortableRemoteObject.narrow(ejbObject,
                      OptimisticLockable.class)).copy();
   }
   else
      throw new java.rmi.RemoteException
            ("entity bean is not OptimisticLockable");
}
```

Figure 89. CopyEntity method of OptimisticLockService Session Bean

The caller of the copyEntity method instantiates a copy of an entity and sets the primary key field(s) for the copy request. The copy object with the search arguments is passed as a parameter to the copy method. The optimistic lock service facade delegates the entity search to the findEntity method of the copy class which invokes the entity's home findByPrimaryKey. A findByPrimaryKey does not exclusively lock the row in the underlying database.

The optimistic lock service redirects the copy request to the found entity bean. The copy method of the entity implementation instantiates and returns a full blown copy to the facade which returns the serialized copy to the caller. The copy transaction commits.

Copy set to read-only

The copy method of the entity *has* to be set to read-only. To prevent a store at commit (which would update the timestamp via database trigger) we select the 'Const method' checkbox for the copy() method in the Properties panel of the bean (VisualAge for Java). For a detailed discussion see 11.1.1, "Read-only methods" on page 173.

In Figure 90 we show the implementation of the updateEntity method.

```
public void updateEntity(OptimisticLockableEntityCopy entityCopy)
   throws OptimisticLockException, java.rmi.RemoteException {
   EJBObject ejbObject = null;
   try {
      //find entity (read-for-update)
      ejbObject = entityCopy.findEntityForUpdate();
   }
   catch(javax.ejb.FinderException finderExcept) {
      throw new OptimisticLockException();
   }
   if (ejbObject instanceof OptimisticLockable) {
      ((OptimisticLockable)javax.rmi.PortableRemoteObject.narrow
      (ejbObject, OptimisticLockable.class)).update(entityCopy);
   }
   else
      throw new java.rmi.RemoteException
            ("entity bean is not OptimisticLockable");
}
```

Figure 90. UpdateEntity method of OptimisticLockService Session Bean

The caller invokes the updateEntity method to synchronize the (updated) entity copy with the server-side entity state. The OptimisticLockService facade delegates the entity search to the findEntityForUpdate method of the copy class which invokes the entity's home custom finder passing the primary key fields and the timestamp from the entity copy as parameters.

If the findEntityForUpdate method does not throw a FinderException, this means that no other transaction has changed the entity state in the meantime. The optimistic lock service redirects the update request to the found entity bean. The update method of the entity implementation synchronizes the entity state with the copy. The optimistic lock service then implicitly commits the update transaction, and the database trigger updates the timestamp.

If the findEntityForUpdate method throws a FinderException, this means that the EJB does not exist anymore, or that another transaction has changed the entity state reflected by the timestamp. In this case, the Optimistic lock service throws an OptimisticLockException and the transaction rolls back.

> **Update not set to read-only**
>
> The update method of the entity *has not* been set to read-only. To enforce a store at commit (which updates the timestamp via database trigger) we do not select the 'Const method' checkbox for the update(OptimisticLockableEntityCopy) method in the Properties panel of the bean (VisualAge for Java). For a detailed discussion see 11.1.1, "Read-only methods" on page 173.
>
> To prevent database deadlocks we recommend that you implement the custom finder with a SELECT FOR UPDATE. A select for update acquires an exclusive lock on the corresponding row. For a detailed discussion see 11.1.3, "Database deadlocks" on page 174.

10.3.5 Sample code

In this section we show the source for an optimistic lockable Customer entity bean. Customer has three persistent fields: customerId, name and lastModified (java.sql.Timestamp).

In Figure 91 we show the copy method implementation of CustomerBean. The copy method creates a copy of the customer state.

```
public OptimisticLockableEntityCopy copy() {
    OptimisticLockableCustomerCopy copy = new
        OptimisticLockableCustomerCopy(customerId, name, lastModified);
    return copy;
}
```

Figure 91. Copy method implementation of CustomerBean

In Figure 92 we show the update method implementation of CustomerBean. The update method synchronizes the bean state with the customer copy.

```
public void update(OptimisticLockableEntityCopy entityCopy) {
    OptimisticLockableCustomerCopy copy =
        (OptimisticLockableCustomerCopy) entityCopy;
    //update entity fields
    setName(copy.getName());
}
```

Figure 92. Update method implemention of CustomerBean

In Figure 93 we show the creation of the two database triggers (before insert / before update).

```
db2 create trigger cust_ins_timestamp no cascade before insert
   on ITSO.CUSTOMER referencing new as CUST for each row
   mode db2sql set CUST.LASTMODIFIED = CURRENT TIMESTAMP

db2 create trigger cust_upd_timestamp no cascade before update
   on ITSO.CUSTOMER referencing new as CUST for each row
   mode db2sql set CUST.LASTMODIFIED = CURRENT TIMESTAMP
```

Figure 93. Database triggers for timestamp setting

In Figure 94 we show the source for the read-for-update custom finder (finder helper interface and class).

```
public interface CustomerBeanFinderHelper {
   public java.sql.PreparedStatement findByPrimaryKeyForUpdate
       (CustomerKey customerKey, java.sql.Timestamp timestamp)
          throws Exception;
}

public class CustomerBeanFinderObject
       extends com.ibm.vap.finders.VapEJSJDBCFinderObject
       implements CustomerBeanFinderHelper {
   public CustomerBeanFinderObject() {
      super();
   }
   public java.sql.PreparedStatement findByPrimaryKeyForUpdate
       (CustomerKey customerKey, java.sql.Timestamp timestamp)
             throws Exception {
      java.sql.PreparedStatement ps = null;
      ps = getMergedPreparedStatement
        ("T1.customerId = ? and T1.lastmodified = ? FOR UPDATE");
      ps.setString(1, customerKey.customerId);
      ps.setObject(2, timestamp);
      return ps;
   }
}
```

Figure 94. Read-for-update custom finder implementation

In Figure 95 we illustrate the implementation of the Customer copy class.

```
public class OptimisticLockableCustomerCopy
            extends OptimisticLockableEntityCopy {
    private String customerId;
    private String name;
    public OptimisticLockableCustomerCopy(String argCustomerId) {
        super(0);
        customerId = argCustomerId;
    }
    public OptimisticLockableCustomerCopy(String argCustomerId,
            String argName, java.sql.Timestamp argTimestamp) {
        super(argTimestamp);
        customerId = argCustomerId;
        name = argName;
    }
    public javax.ejb.EJBObject findEntity()
        throws java.rmi.RemoteException, javax.ejb.FinderException {
        //get narrowed home reference from base class
        CustomerHome customerHome = (CustomerHome) getHome();
        return customerHome.findByPrimaryKey
                (new CustomerKey(customerId));
    }
    public javax.ejb.EJBObject findEntityForUpdate()
        throws java.rmi.RemoteException, javax.ejb.FinderException {
        //get narrowed home reference from base class
        CustomerHome customerHome = (CustomerHome) getHome();
        return customerHome.findByPrimaryKeyForUpdate
                (new CustomerKey(getCustomerId()), getTimestamp());
    }
    public String getCustomerId()   { return customerId; }
    public String getName()         { return name; }
    protected String getHomeName() { return "Customer"; }
}
```

Figure 95. Implementation of Customer copy class

The constructor OptimisticLockableCustomerCopy(String argCustomerId) is
used to specify the primary key field (customerId) of the customer to copy
(passed as parameter in the copyEntity method of the OptimisticLockService
facade).

10.3.6 Related patterns

The patterns related to the optimistic locking service are EJB session facade
and EJB home factory.

Chapter 11. EJB performance guidelines

In this chapter we discuss database related performance guidelines for EJBs.

11.1 Database access

The following considerations are valid for EJB deployment on IBM WebSphere Advanced.

11.1.1 Read-only methods

The EJB specification does not provide a standard mechanism to allow a container to check if the bean's state has changed within a unit of work.

As an IBM extension to the EJB specification, VisualAge for Java allows the bean developer to define the method types (read-only or update). With the Const Method checkbox in the control descriptor of the bean's Properties panel (Method screen), a selected checkbox means read-only, and non-checked is an update method. The default is update. See Figure 96.

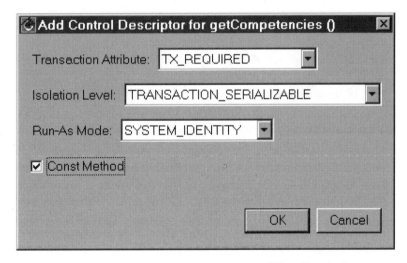

Figure 96. Read-only flag in the control descriptor of VisualAge for Java

When deploying the EJB on IBM WebSphere Advanced Edition, the container runtime only stores a bean's state if at least one non read-only (update) method has been invoked during a transaction. This eliminates unnecessary SQL UPDATE at commit time, for example for getters that do not change the entity state.

When an update (non read-only) method is invoked on a bean and the bean is not active, the container runtime will load the bean using the Persister loadForUpdate method. This method will (typically) acquire a lock on the bean's state in the underlying data store.

11.1.2 Transaction life cycle

Locking mechanisms are used by database managers to handle resource allocation among many users without compromising data integrity. While necessary and valuable, locking tends to impact the ability to handle multiple requests for the same data resource concurrently.

As a general rule transactions should not span user think-time. A transaction lives between the reception of a user request and the return of the response. A user should not control transaction demarcation.

The introduction of the session facade design pattern supports this locking strategy. The facade handles the transaction demarcation explicitly (TX_BEAN_MANAGED) or delegates the transaction life cycle to the container (TX_REQUIRES) which implicitly starts and commits (or rollbacks) a transaction.

The first, and least exclusive alternative is optimistic locking. With optimistic locking updates are not actually attempted until all business conditions are met. The side affect of this approach is that the original data values must be re-validated before updates are actually applied. For a detailed discussion see 10.3, "Optimistic locking pattern" on page 162.

11.1.3 Database deadlocks

The implementation of the withdraw method (see Figure 97) leads to a database deadlock when two clients concurrently try to withdraw from the same account. The assumption is that the invoked withdraw method which is part of a session facade and Account.withdraw both have transaction attribute TX_REQUIRES and isolation level TRANSACTION_SERIALIZABLE or TRANSACTION_REPEATABLE_READ. Other transaction attribute / isolation level combinations probably do not run into deadlocks, but could lead to data inconsistency.

The deadlock detection is database implementation specific. In DB2 UDB both threads are waiting until lock time-out is reached. Then the database manager aborts one of the threads with an "SQL0911N The current transaction has been rolled back" exception. The other thread continues and will end (eventually) correctly.

```
public void withdraw(String accountId, java.math.BigDecimal amount)
   throws javax.ejb.FinderException, java.rmi.RemoteException {
   Account account = getAccountHome().findByPrimaryKey(new
   AccountKey(accountId));
   account.withdraw(amount);
}
```

Figure 97. Withdraw from account with deadlock potential

The Account's home findByPrimaryKey methods activates and loads the account bean for the first transaction with a SQL SELECT from the database (read-only). The finder of the second transaction can concurrently load the same bean state, because the database manager has acquired a shared (read) lock on this row. Both transactions now withdraw the amount from the same balance. Because Account.withdraw is a non-const (update) method both transactions try to store the account's state, including the wrong balance, at commit time. The database manager responsible for concurrency attempts to convert their shared locks to exclusive locks. This leads to a deadlock. Both transactions are waiting the termination of the other. The database manager resolves the awaiting conflict when the locks time out and rollback one of them.

Depending on the lock time-out parameter, both transactions can be blocked for a reasonable time.

Figure 98 illustrates the solution to prevent deadlocks. The account is loaded via a SELECT FOR UPDATE (custom finder in AccountHome). Now the database manager serializes the two transactions at bean load time. The account state for the second transaction cannot be loaded while the first transaction is still active. Both transactions can (eventually) run correctly.

```
public void withdraw(String accountId, java.math.BigDecimal amount)
    throws javax.ejb.FinderException, java.rmi.RemoteException {
    Account account = getAccountHome().findForUpdate(accountId));
    account.withdraw(amount);
}
```

Figure 98. Withdraw from account without deadlock potential

The Client Console of WebSphere Advanced Enterprise Edition 3.02 has a checkbox 'Find for update' in the Enterprise Bean notebook's Advanced tab. Checking this box means: the findByPrimaryKey method of all homes are invoked with the FOR UPDATE clause. To prevent unnecessary serializations for read-only transactions, we have decided to implement a custom finder.

It is worth to say that when an update (non-const) is invoked on a bean and the bean is not active, the container runtime will implicitly load the bean using the Persister loadForUpdate. However, with the preferred Session Facade pattern a bean will obviously be loaded via home finder. This means that the non-const flag has no influence for the bean load.

11.1.4 Caching

The EJB specification define two levels of caching, commit options A and C. These commit options are implemented in WebSphere Application Server.

11.1.4.1 Commit options and database connections

WebSphere Advanced Edition supports commit option A (entity beans cached between transactions) and commit option C (entity beans not cached between transaction). Commit option A dramatically reduces the number of database accesses in comparison to option C, but has some concerns. This chapter describes the advantages and disadvantages of the options and compares the state transitions, activation and passivation.

A concurrency control mechanism is needed by the container, or the underlying database, to control concurrent access to entity bean instances. The aim of the container's concurrency control and caching mechanism is to allow concurrent transactions to access a single entity bean instance in such a way that concurrent requests are serialized with respect to their access to the bean instance. For IBM WebSphere Advanced, the container concurrency control/caching mechanism performs concurrency control in object space for beans cached between transactions (commit option A) and delegates concurrency control to the database for beans that are not cached (commit option C).

11.1.4.2 Entities not cached between transactions (option C)

In IBM WebSphere Advanced when a bean is not cached between transactions there is always a transaction associated with the bean's persistent state at the database; this means that the transaction is used to load the bean's persistent state when it first joined the transaction. The database will ensure that this transaction is isolated with respect to other database transactions by locking the bean's persistent state. What type of locks are taken, and the duration of the locks are all questions that you must consider in order to understand what type of behavior to expect from this strategy.

11.1.4.3 Entities cached between transactions (option A)

IBM WebSphere Advanced Edition supports commit option A. This is done at the enterprise bean level by specifying the database access level. Option A is activated by selecting **Exclusive** on the database access parameter.

In this case, transaction isolation is ensured by the container instead of being delegated to the database. Because of its exclusive access to the database, the container caches the enterprise beans and does not systematically load and store the bean state between transactions. It improves performances but prevents other applications from sharing the same database records.

Appendix A. Special notices

This publication is intended to help application developers and architects to design e-business types of applications. The information in this publication is not intended as the specification of any programming interfaces that are provided by VisualAge for Java or IBM WebSphere Advanced Edition. See the PUBLICATIONS section of the IBM Programming Announcement for VisualAge for Java or IBM WebSphere Advanced Edition for more information about what publications are considered to be product documentation.

References in this publication to IBM products, programs or services do not imply that IBM intends to make these available in all countries in which IBM operates. Any reference to an IBM product, program, or service is not intended to state or imply that only IBM's product, program, or service may be used. Any functionally equivalent program that does not infringe any of IBM's intellectual property rights may be used instead of the IBM product, program or service.

Information in this book was developed in conjunction with use of the equipment specified, and is limited in application to those specific hardware and software products and levels.

IBM may have patents or pending patent applications covering subject matter in this document. The furnishing of this document does not give you any license to these patents. You can send license inquiries, in writing, to the IBM Director of Licensing, IBM Corporation, North Castle Drive, Armonk, NY 10504-1785.

Licensees of this program who wish to have information about it for the purpose of enabling: (i) the exchange of information between independently created programs and other programs (including this one) and (ii) the mutual use of the information which has been exchanged, should contact IBM Corporation, Dept. 600A, Mail Drop 1329, Somers, NY 10589 USA.

Such information may be available, subject to appropriate terms and conditions, including in some cases, payment of a fee.

The information contained in this document has not been submitted to any formal IBM test and is distributed AS IS. The use of this information or the implementation of any of these techniques is a customer responsibility and depends on the customer's ability to evaluate and integrate them into the customer's operational environment. While each item may have been reviewed by IBM for accuracy in a specific situation, there is no guarantee that the same or similar results will be obtained elsewhere. Customers attempting to adapt these techniques to their own environments do so at their own risk.

Any pointers in this publication to external Web sites are provided for convenience only and do not in any manner serve as an endorsement of these Web sites.

The following terms are trademarks of the International Business Machines Corporation in the United States and/or other countries:

IBM ®	CICS
DB2	MQSeries
SecureWay	VisualAge
WebSphere	

The following terms are trademarks of other companies:

Tivoli, Manage. Anything. Anywhere.,The Power To Manage., Anything. Anywhere.,TME, NetView, Cross-Site, Tivoli Ready, Tivoli Certified, Planet Tivoli, and Tivoli Enterprise are trademarks or registered trademarks of Tivoli Systems Inc., an IBM company, in the United States, other countries, or both. In Denmark, Tivoli is a trademark licensed from Kjøbenhavns Sommer - Tivoli A/S.

C-bus is a trademark of Corollary, Inc. in the United States and/or other countries.

Java and all Java-based trademarks and logos are trademarks or registered trademarks of Sun Microsystems, Inc. in the United States and/or other countries.

Microsoft, Windows, Windows NT, and the Windows logo are trademarks of Microsoft Corporation in the United States and/or other countries.

PC Direct is a trademark of Ziff Communications Company in the United States and/or other countries and is used by IBM Corporation under license.

ActionMedia, LANDesk, MMX, Pentium and ProShare are trademarks of Intel Corporation in the United States and/or other countries.

UNIX is a registered trademark in the United States and other countries licensed exclusively through The Open Group.

SET and the SET logo are trademarks owned by SET Secure Electronic Transaction LLC.

Other company, product, and service names may be trademarks or service marks of others.

Appendix B. Related publications

The publications listed in this section are considered particularly suitable for a more detailed discussion of the topics covered in this redbook.

B.1 IBM Redbooks publications

For information on ordering these publications see "How to get IBM Redbooks" on page 185.

- *Servlet and JSP Programming with IBM WebSphere Studio and VisualAge for Java*, SG24-5755
- *Patterns for e-business: User-to-Business Patterns for Topology 1 and 2 using WebSphere Advanced Edition*, SG24-5864
- *IBM WebSphere Performance Pack: Load Balancing with IBM SecureWay Network Dispatcher*, SG24-5858
- *WebSphere Version 3 Performance Tuning Guide*, SG24-5657
- *VisualAge for Java Enterprise Version 3: Persistence Builder with GUIs, Servlets, and Java Server Pages*, SG24-5426
- *The XML Files: Using XML and XSL with IBM WebSphere V3.0*, SG24-5479
- *Enterprise JavaBeans Development Using VisualAge for Java*, SG24-5429

B.2 IBM Redbooks collections

Redbooks are also available on the following CD-ROMs. Click the CD-ROMs button at http://www.redbooks.ibm.com/ for information about all the CD ROMs offered, updates and formats.

CD-ROM Title	Collection Kit Number
System/390 Redbooks Collection	SK2T-2177
Networking and Systems Management Redbooks Collection	SK2T-6022
Transaction Processing and Data Management Redbooks Collection	SK2T-8038
Lotus Redbooks Collection	SK2T-8039
Tivoli Redbooks Collection	SK2T-8044
AS/400 Redbooks Collection	SK2T-2849
Netfinity Hardware and Software Redbooks Collection	SK2T-8046
RS/6000 Redbooks Collection (BkMgr)	SK2T-8040
RS/6000 Redbooks Collection (PDF Format)	SK2T-8043
Application Development Redbooks Collection	SK2T-8037
IBM Enterprise Storage and Systems Management Solutions	SK3T-3694

B.3 Other resources

This publication is also relevant as a further information source:

- *Design Patterns: Elements of Reusable Object-Oriented Software*, Erich Gamma, Richard Helm, Ralph Johnson, and John Vlissides, published by Addison-Wesley Professional Computing Series, ISBN 0-201-63361, 1995 (IBM form number SR28-5629)

B.4 Referenced Web sites

These Web sites are also relevant as further information sources:

- http://www.ibm.com/software/developer/web/patterns/
- http://www.w3.org
- http://www.javaworld.com/

How to get IBM Redbooks

This section explains how both customers and IBM employees can find out about IBM Redbooks, redpieces, and CD-ROMs. A form for ordering books and CD-ROMs by fax or e-mail is also provided.

- **Redbooks Web Site** http://www.redbooks.ibm.com/

  Search for, view, download, or order hardcopy/CD-ROM Redbooks from the Redbooks Web site. Also read redpieces and download additional materials (code samples or diskette/CD-ROM images) from this Redbooks site.

  Redpieces are Redbooks in progress; not all Redbooks become redpieces and sometimes just a few chapters will be published this way. The intent is to get the information out much quicker than the formal publishing process allows.

- **E-mail Orders**

  Send orders by e-mail including information from the IBM Redbooks fax order form to:

	e-mail address
In United States	usib6fpl@ibmmail.com
Outside North America	Contact information is in the "How to Order" section at this site: http://www.elink.ibmlink.ibm.com/pbl/pbl

- **Telephone Orders**

United States (toll free)	1-800-879-2755
Canada (toll free)	1-800-IBM-4YOU
Outside North America	Country coordinator phone number is in the "How to Order" section at this site: http://www.elink.ibmlink.ibm.com/pbl/pbl

- **Fax Orders**

United States (toll free)	1-800-445-9269
Canada	1-403-267-4455
Outside North America	Fax phone number is in the "How to Order" section at this site: http://www.elink.ibmlink.ibm.com/pbl/pbl

This information was current at the time of publication, but is continually subject to change. The latest information may be found at the Redbooks Web site.

IBM Intranet for Employees

IBM employees may register for information on workshops, residencies, and Redbooks by accessing the IBM Intranet Web site at http://w3.itso.ibm.com/ and clicking the ITSO Mailing List button. Look in the Materials repository for workshops, presentations, papers, and Web pages developed and written by the ITSO technical professionals; click the Additional Materials button. Employees may access MyNews at http://w3.ibm.com/ for redbook, residency, and workshop announcements.

IBM Redbooks fax order form

Please send me the following:

Title	Order Number	Quantity

First name _____ Last name _____

Company _____

Address _____

City _____ Postal code _____ Country _____

Telephone number _____ Telefax number _____ VAT number _____

☐ Invoice to customer number _____

☐ Credit card number _____

Credit card expiration date _____ Card issued to _____ Signature _____

We accept American Express, Diners, Eurocard, Master Card, and Visa. Payment by credit card not available in all countries. Signature mandatory for credit card payment.

Glossary

This glossary defines terms and abbreviations that are used in this book. If you do not find the term you are looking for, refer to the *IBM Dictionary of Computing*, New York: McGraw-Hill, 1994.

This glossary includes terms and definitions from the *American National Standard Dictionary for Information Systems*, ANSI X3.172-1990, copyright 1990 by the American National Standards Institute (ANSI). Copies may be purchased from the American National Standards Institute, 1430 Broadway, New York, New York 10018.

A

abstract class. A class that provides common behavior across a set of subclasses but is not itself designed to have instances that work. An abstract class represents a concept; classes derived from it represent implementations of the concept. See also *base class*.

access application. Generated by the Data Access Builder for each schema mapping, an executable GUI that provides access to the database using the other classes generated for the mapping.

accessor methods. Methods that an object provides to define the interface to its instance variables. The accessor method to return the value of an instance variable is called a *get* method or *getter* method, and the accessor method to assign a value to an instance variable is called a *set* method or *setter* method.

applet. A Java program designed to run within a Web browser. Contrast with application.

application. In Java programming, a self-contained, stand-alone Java program that includes a main() method. Contrast with applet.

application server. A server program that allows the installation of application specific software components, in a manner so that they can be remotely invoked, usually by some for of remote object method call.

argument. A data element, or value, included as a bean in a method call. Arguments provide additional information that the called method can use to perform the requested operation.

attribute. A specification of a property of a bean. For example, a customer bean could have a name attribute and an address attribute. An attribute can itself be a bean with its own behavior and attributes. In the Data Access Builder, the aspect of a schema mapping that represents a column in a database table.

B

base class. A class from which other classes or beans are derived. A base class may itself be derived from another base class. See also *abstract class*.

bean. A definition or instance of a JavaBeans component. See also *JavaBeans*.

BeanInfo. (1) A companion class for a bean that defines a set of methods that can be accessed to retrieve information on the bean's properties, events, and methods. (2) In the VisualAge for Java IDE, a page in the class browser that provides bean information.

bean-managed persistence (BMP). When an Enterprise JavaBeans performs its own long-term state management.

beans palette. In the Visual Composition Editor, a two-column pane that contains prefabricated beans that you can select and manipulate to create programs. The left column contains categories of beans, and the right column contains beans for the selected category. The default set of beans generally represents JDK AWT components. You can add your own categories and beans to the beans palette.

break point. A point in a computer program where the execution can be halted.

browser. (1) In VisualAge for Java, a window that provides information on program elements. There are browsers for projects, packages, classes, methods, and interfaces. (2) An Internet-based tool that loto users browse Web sites.

C

C++ Access Builder. A VisualAge for Java Enterprise tool that generates beans to access C and C++ DLLs.

category. In the Visual Composition Editor, a selectable grouping of beans represented by an icon in the left-most column. Selecting a category displays the beans belonging to that category in the next column. See also *beans palette*.

CICS Access Builder. A VisualAge for Java Enterprise tool that generates beans to access CICS transactions through the CICS Gateway for Java and CICS Client.

CICS Client. A server program that processes CICS ECI calls, forwarding transaction requests to a CICS program running on a host.

CICS ECI. An API that provides C and C++ programs with procedural access to transactions.

CICS Gateway for Java. A server program that processes Java ECI calls and forwards CICS ECI calls to the CICS Client.

class. An aggregate that defines properties, operations, and behavior for all instances of that aggregate.

class hierarchy. The relationships between classes that share a single inheritance. All Java classes inherit from the Object class.

class library. A collection of classes.

class method. See *method*.

CLASSPATH. In your deployment environment, the environment variable that specifies the directories in which to look for class and resource files.

client/server. The model of interaction in distributed data processing where a program at one location sends a request to a program at another location and awaits a response. The requesting

program is called a *client*, and the answering program is called a *server*.

client-side server proxy. Generated by the RMI Access Builder, a local representative of a remote bean. This proxy provides access to the operations of the server bean, allowing a Java client to work with it as if it were the server bean. See also *proxy bean* and *server-side server proxy*.

Class Browser. In the VisualAge for Java IDE, a tool used to browse the classes loaded in the workspace.

collection. A set of features in which each feature is an object.

commit. The operation that ends a unit of work and updates the database such that other processes can access any changes made.

Common Object Request Broker Architecture (CORBA). A middleware specification which defines a software bus—the Object Request Broker (ORB)—that provides the infrastructure.

communications area (COMMAREA). In a CICS transaction program, a group of records that describes both the format and volume of data used.

component model. An architecture and an API that allows developers to define reusable segments of code that can be combined to create a program. VisualAge for Java uses the JavaBeans component model.

composite bean. A bean that is composed of a bean and one or more subbeans. A composite bean can contain visual beans, nonvisual beans, or both. See also *nonvisual bean, bean,* and *visual bean*.

concrete class. A subclass of an abstract class that is a specialization of the abstract class.

connection. In the Visual Composition Editor, a visual link between two components that represents the relationship between the components. Each connection has a source, a target, and other properties. See also *event-to-method connection, event-to-property connection, parameter connection, property-to-method connection,* and *property-to-property connection*.

console. In VisualAge for Java, the window that acts as the standard input (System.in) and standard output (System.out) device for programs running in the VisualAge for Java IDE.

container-managed persistence (CMP). When an Enterprise JavaBeans server manages a bean's long-term state.

construction from parts. A software development technology in which applications are assembled from existing and reusable software components, known as *parts*. In VisualAge for Java, parts are called *beans*.

constructor. A special class method that has the same name as the class and is used to construct and possibly initialize objects of its class type.

container. A component that can hold other components. In Java, examples of containers include applets, frames, and dialogs. In the Visual Composition Editor, containers can be graphically represented and generated.

current edition. The edition of a program element that is currently in the workspace. See also *open edition*.

cursor. A database control structure used by the Data Access Builder to point to a specific row within some ordered set of rows and to retrieve rows from a set, possibly making updates or deletions.

D

data abstraction. A data type with a private representation and a public set of operations. The Java language uses the concept of classes to implement data abstraction.

Data Access Builder. A VisualAge for Java Enterprise tool that generates beans to access and manipulate the content of JDBC/ODBC-compliant relational databases.

DB2 for MVS/ESA. An IBM relational database management system for the MVS operating system.

double-byte character set (DBCS). A set of characters in which each character is represented by 2 bytes. Languages such as Japanese, Chinese, and Korean, which contain more symbols than can be represented by 256 code points, require

double-byte character sets. Compare with *single-byte character set*.

Distributed Computing Environment (DCE). Adopted by the computer industry as a de facto standard for distributed computing. DCE allows computers from a variety of vendors to communicate transparently and share resources such as computing power, files, printers, and other objects in the network.

Distributed Component Object Model (DCOM). A protocol that enables software components to communicate directly over a network in a reliable, secure, and efficient manner. Previously called "Network OLE," DCOM is designed for use across multiple network transports, including Internet protocols such as HTTP. DCOM is based on the Open Software Foundation's DCE-RPC specification and works with both Java applets and ActiveX components through its use of the Component Object Model (COM).

DMZ. Demilitarized Zone.

DTD. Document type definition.

dynamic link library (DLL). A file containing executable code and data bound to a program at run time rather than at link time. The C++ Access Builder generates beans and C++ wrappers that let your Java programs access C++ DLLs.

E

edition. A specific "cut" of a program element. VisualAge for Java supports multiple editions of program elements. See also *current edition, open edition*, and *versioned edition*.

encapsulation. The hiding of a software object's internal representation. The object provides an interface that queries and manipulates the data without exposing its underlying structure.

enterprise access builders. In VisualAge for Java Enterprise, a set of code-generation tools. See also *C++ Access Builder, CICS Access Builder, Data Access Builder*, and *RMI Access Builder*.

Enterprise JavaBeans (EJB). A server component developed by SUN Microsystems.

event. An action by a user program, or a specification of a notification that may trigger specific behavior. In JDK 1.1, events notify the relevant listener classes to take appropriate actions.

event-to-method connection. A connection from an event generated by a bean to a method of another bean. When the connected event occurs, the method is executed. See also *connection*.

event-to-property connection. A connection that changes the value of a property when a certain event occurs. See also *connection*.

F

feature. (1) A major component of a software product that can be installed separately. (2) In VisualAge for Java, a method, field, or event that is available from a bean's interface and to which other beans can connect.

field. A data object in a class. For example, a customer class could have a name field and an address field. A field can itself be an object with its own behavior and fields. By default, a field, in contrast to a property, does not support event notification.

free-form surface. The large open area of the Visual Composition Editor where you can work with visual and nonvisual beans. You add, remove, and connect beans on the free-form surface.

framework. A set of cooperative classes with strong connections that provide a template for development.

G

garbage collection. A Smalltalk process for periodically identifying unreferenced objects and deallocating their memory.

gateway. A host computer that connects networks that communicate in different languages. For example, a gateway connects a company's LAN to the Internet.

graphical user interface (GUI). A type of interface that enables users to communicate with a program by manipulating graphical features, rather than by entering commands. Typically, a graphical user interface includes a combination of graphics, pointing devices, menu bars and other menus, overlapping windows, and icons.

H

hypertext. Text in a document that contains a hidden link to other text. You can click a mouse on a hypertext word and it will take you to the text designated in the link. Hypertext is used in Windows help programs and CD encyclopedias to jump to related references elsewhere within the same document. Hypertext can link–using HTTP over the Web–to any Web document in the world, with only a single mouse click.

Hypertext Markup Language (HTML). The basic language that is used to build hypertext documents on the World Wide Web. It is used in basic, plain ASCII-text documents, but when those documents are interpreted (*rendered*) by a Web browser such as Netscape, the document can display formatted text, color, a variety of fonts, graphics images, special effects, hypertext jumps to other Internet locations, and information forms.

Hypertext Transfer Protocol (HTTP). The protocol for moving hypertext files across the Internet. Requires an HTTP client program on one end, and an HTTP server program on the other end.

I

inheritance. (1) A mechanism by which an object class can use the attributes, relationships, and methods defined in more abstract classes related to it (its base classes). (2) An object-oriented programming technique that allows you to use existing classes as bases for creating other classes.

instance. Synonym for *object*, a particular instantiation of a data type.

Integrated Development Environment (IDE). In VisualAge for Java, the set of windows that provide the user with access to development tools. The primary windows are Workbench, Log, Console, Debugger, and Repository Explorer.

interchange file. A file that you can export from VisualAge for Java that contains information about selected projects or packages. This file can then be imported into any VisualAge for Java session.

interface. A set of methods that can be accessed by any class in the class hierarchy. The Interface page in the Workbench lists all interfaces in the workspace.

Internet. The vast collection of interconnected networks that use TCP/IP and evolved from the ARPANET of the late 1960s and early 1970s.

intranet. A private *network,* inside a company or organization, that uses the same kinds of software that you would find on the public *Internet.* Many of the tools used on the Internet are being used in private networks; for example, many companies have Web servers that are available only to employees.

Internet Protocol (IP). The rules that provide basic Internet functions. See *Transmission Control Protocol/Internet Protocol.*

IP number. An Internet address that is a unique number consisting of four parts separated by dots, sometimes called a *dotted quad* (for example: 198.204.112.1). Every Internet computer has an IP number, and most computers also have one or more domain names that are plain language substitutes for the dotted quad.

J

Java. A programming language invented by Sun Microsystems that is specifically designed for writing programs that can be safely downloaded to your computer through the Internet and immediately run without fear of viruses or other harm to your computer or files. Using small Java programs (called *applets*), Web pages can include functions such as animation, calculators, and other fancy tricks. We can expect to see a huge variety of features added to the Web through Java, because you can write a Java program to do almost anything a regular computer program can do and then include that Java program in a Web page.

Java archive (JAR). A platform-independent file format that groups many files into one. JAR files are used for compression, reduced download time, and security. Because the JAR format is written in Java, JAR files are fully extensible.

JavaBeans. In JDK 1.1, the specification that defines the platform-neutral component model used to represent parts. Instances of JavaBeans (often called beans) may have methods, properties, and events.

Java Database Connectivity (JDBC). In JDK 1.1, the specification that defines an API that enables programs to access databases that comply with this standard.

Java Naming and Directory Interace (JNDI). The Java standard API for accessing directory services, such as LDAP, COS Naming, and others.

Java Native Interface (JNI). In JDK 1.1, the specification that defines a standard naming and calling convention so that the Java virtual machine can locate and invoke methods written in a language different from Java. See also *native method.*

JSP. JavaServer Pages.

JTA. Java Transaction API.

JTS. The Java Transaction Service based on the CORBA Transaction Service which provides a way for middleware vendors to build interoperable transactional middleware.

JVM. Java Virtual Machine.

K

keyword. A predefined word, reserved for Java, that cannot be used as an identifier.

L

LDAP. Lightweight Directory Access Protocol for accessing X.500 directories.

legacy code. Existing code that a user might have. Legacy applications often have character-based, nongraphical user interfaces. Usually they are written in a non-object-oriented language, such as C or COBOL.

listener. In JDK 1.1, a class that receives and handles events.

local area network (LAN). A computer network located on a user's establishment within a limited geographical area. A LAN typically consists of one or more server machines providing services to a number of client workstations.

log. In VisualAge for Java, the window that displays messages and warnings during development.

M

mapping. See *schema mapping*.

member. (1) A data object in a structure or a union. (2) In Java, classes and structures can also contain functions and types as members.

method. A fragment of Java code within a class that can be invoked and passed a set of parameters to perform a specific task.

method call. A communication from one object to another that requests the receiving object to execute a method. A method call consists of a method name that indicates the requested method and the arguments to be used in executing the method. The method call always returns some object to the requesting object as the result of performing the method. Synonym for *message*.

message. A request from one object that the receiving object implement a method. Because data is encapsulated and not directly accessible, a message is the only way to send data from one object to another. Each message specifies the name of the receiving object, the method to be implemented, and any arguments the method needs for implementation. Synonym for *method call*.

model. A nonvisual bean that represents the state and behavior of an object, such as a customer or an account. Contrast with *view*.

MVC. Model-View-Controller.

N

native method. Method written in a language other than Java that can be called by a Java object through the JNI specification.

named package. In the VisualAge for Java IDE, a package that has been explicitly named and created.

nonvisual bean. In the Visual Composition Editor, a bean that has no visual representation at run time. A nonvisual bean typically represents some real-world object that exists in the business environment. Compare with *model*. Contrast with *view* and *visual bean*.

notification framework. In JDK 1.1, a set of classes that implement the *notifier/listener* protocol. The notification framework is the base of the construction from beans technology (Visual Composition Editor).

O

object. (1) A computer representation of something that a user can work with to perform a task. An object can appear as text or an icon. (2) A collection of data and methods that operate on that data, which together represent a logical entity in the system. In object-oriented programming, objects are grouped into classes that share common data definitions and methods. Each object in the class is said to be an instance of the class. (3) An instance of an object class consisting of attributes, a data structure, and operational methods. It can represent a person, place, thing, event, or concept. Each instance has the same properties, attributes, and methods as other instances of the object class, although it has unique values assigned to its attributes.

object class. A template for defining the attributes and methods of an object. An object class can contain other object classes. An individual representation of an object class is called an *object*.

object factory. A nonvisual bean capable of dynamically creating new instances of a specified bean. For example, during the execution of an application, an object factory can create instances of a new class to collect the data being generated.

object-oriented programming (OOP). A programming approach based on the concepts of data abstraction and inheritance. Unlike procedural programming techniques, object-oriented programming concentrates on those data objects that constitute the problem and how they are manipulated, not on how something is accomplished.

Object Request Broker (ORB). A CORBA term designating the means by which objects transparently make requests and receive responses from objects, whether they are local or remote.

ODBC driver. A DLL that implements ODBC function calls and interacts with a data source.

Open Database Connectivity (ODBC). A Microsoft developed C database API that allows access to database management systems calling callable SQL, which does not require the use of an SQL preprocessor. In addition, ODBC provides an architecture that allows users to add modules (database drivers) that link the application to their choice of database management systems at run time. Applications no longer need to be directly linked to the modules of all the database management systems that are supported.

open edition. An edition of a program element that can still be modified; that is, the edition has not been versioned. An open edition may reside in the workspace as well as in the repository.

operation. A method or service that can be requested of an object.

OSE. Open servlet engine.

overloading. An object-oriented programming technique that allows redefinition of methods when the methods are used with class types.

P

package. A program element that contains related classes and interfaces.

palette. See *beans palette*.

parameter connection. A connection that satisfies a parameter of an action or method by supplying either a property's value or the return value of an action, method, or script. The parameter is always the source of the connection. See also *connection*.

parent class. The class from which another bean or class inherits data, methods, or both.

part. An existing, reusable software component. In VisualAge for Java, all parts created with the Visual Composition Editor conform to the JavaBeans component model and are referred to as beans. See also *nonvisual bean* and *visual bean*. Compare with *Class Editor* and *Composition Editor*.

PDA. Personal Digital Assistant.

primitive bean. A basic building block of other beans. A primitive bean can be relatively complex in terms of the function it provides.

private. In Java, an access modifier associated with a class member. It allows only the class itself to access the member.

process. A collection of code, data, and other system resources, including at least one thread of execution, that performs a data processing task.

program. In VisualAge for Java, a term that refers to both Java applets and applications.

project. In VisualAge for Java, the topmost kind of program element. A project contains Java packages.

promote features. Make features of a subbean available to be used for making connections. This applies to subbeans that are to be included in other beans, for example, a subbean consisting of three push buttons on a panel. If this sample subbean is placed in a frame, the features of the push buttons would have to be promoted to make them available from within the frame.

property. An initial setting or characteristic of a bean; for example, a name, font, text, or positional characteristic.

property sheet. In the Visual Composition Editor, a set of name-value pairs that specify the initial appearance and other bean characteristics. A bean's property sheet can be viewed from the Properties secondary window.

property-to-method connection. A connection that calls a method whenever a property's value changes. It is similar to an event-to-method connection because the property's event ID is used to notify the method when the value of the property changes. See also *connection*.

property-to-property connection. A connection from a property of one bean to a property of another bean. When one property is updated, the other property is updated automatically. See also *connection*.

property-to-method connection. A connection from a property of a bean to a method. When the property undergoes a state change, the method is called. See also *connection*.

protected. In Java, an access modifier associated with a class member. It allows the class itself, subclasses, and all classes in the same package to access the member.

protocol. (1) The set of all messages to which an object will respond. (2) Specification of the structure and meaning (the semantics) of messages that are exchanged between a client and a server. (3) Computer rules that provide uniform specifications so that computer hardware and operating systems can communicate. It is similar to the way that mail, in countries around the world, is addressed in the same basic format so that postal workers know where to find the recipient's address, the sender's return address, and the postage stamp. Regardless of the underlying language, the basic protocols remain the same.

prototype. A method declaration or definition that includes both the return type of the method and the types of its arguments.

proxy bean. A group of client-side and server-side objects that represent a remote server bean. The top-level class that implements the proxy bean is the client-side server proxy. See also *client-side server proxy* and *server-side server proxy*.

R

Remote Method Invocation (RMI). In JDK 1.1, the API that enables you to write distributed Java programs, allowing methods of remote Java objects to be accessed from other Java virtual machines.

remote object instance manager. Creates and manages instances of RMI server beans through their associated server-side server proxies.

repository. In VisualAge for Java, the storage area, separate from the workspace, that contains all editions (both open and versioned) of all program elements that have ever been in the workspace, including the current editions that are in the workspace. You can add editions of program elements to the workspace from the repository.

Repository Explorer. In VisualAge for Java, the window from which you can view and compare editions of program elements that are in the repository.

resource file. A noncode file that can be referred to from your Java program in VisualAge for Java. Examples include graphics and audio files.

RMI Access Builder. A VisualAge for Java Enterprise tool that generates proxy beans and associated classes and interfaces so you can distribute code for remote access, enabling Java-to-Java solutions.

RMI compiler. The compiler that generates stub and skeleton files that facilitate RMI communication. This compiler can be automatically invoked by the RMI Access Builder or from the Tools menu item.

RMI registry. A server program that allows remote clients to get a reference to a server bean.

roll back. The process of restoring data changed by SQL statements to the state at its last commit point.

S

schema. In the Data Access Builder, the representation of the database that will be mapped.

schema mapping. In the Data Access Builder, a set of definitions for all attributes matching all columns for your database table, view, or SQL statement. The mapping contains the information required by the Data Access Builder to generate Java classes.

Scrapbook. In VisualAge for Java, the window from which you can write and test fragments of code, without having to define an encompassing class or method.

server. A computer that provides services to multiple users or workstations in a network; for example, a file server, a print server, or a mail server.

server bean. The bean that is distributed using RMI services and deployed on a server.

server-side server proxy. Generated by the RMI Access Builder, a companion class to the client-side server proxy, facilitating client-side server proxy communication over RMI. See also *client-side server proxy* and *proxy bean*.

service. A specific behavior that an object is responsible for exhibiting.

single-byte character set. A set of characters in which each character is represented by a 1- byte code.

SmartGuide. In IBM software products, an interface that guides you through performing common tasks.

SQL predicate. The conditional part of an SQL statement.

sticky. In the Visual Composition Editor, the mode that enables an application developer to add multiple beans of the same class (for example, three push buttons) without going back and forth between the beans palette and the free-form surface.

stored procedure. A procedure that is part of a relational database. The Data Access Builder can generate Java code that accesses stored procedures.

superclass. See *abstract class* and *base class*.

T

Transmission Control Protocol/Internet Protocol (TCP/IP). The basic programming foundation that carries computer messages around the globe through the Internet. The suite of protocols that defines the Internet. Originally designed for the UNIX operating system, TCP/IP software is now available for every major kind of computer operating system. To be truly on the Internet, your computer must have TCP/IP software.

tear-off property. A property that a developer has exposed to work with as though it were a stand-alone bean.

thread. A unit of execution within a process.

tool bar. The strip of icons along the top of the free-form surface. The tool bar contains tools to help an application developer construct composite beans.

transaction. In a CICS program, an event that queries or modifies a database that resides on a CICS server.

type. In VisualAge for Java, a generic term for a class or interface.

U

UDB. Universal database (as in DB2 UDB).

Unicode. A character coding system designed to support the interchange, processing, and display of the written texts of the diverse languages of the modern world. Unicode characters are normally encoded using 16-bit integral unsigned numbers.

uniform resource locator (URL). A standard identifier for a resource on the World Wide Web, used by Web browsers to initiate a connection. The URL includes the communications protocol to use, the name of the server, and path information identifying the objects to be retrieved on the server. A URL looks like this:

http://www.matisse.net/seminars.html

or telnet://well.sf.ca.us.br

or news:new.newusers.question.br

user interface (UI). (1) The hardware, software, or both that enables a user to interact with a computer. (2) The visual presentation and its underlying software with which a user interacts.

V

variable. (1) A storage place within an object for a data feature. The data feature is an object, such as number or date, stored as an attribute of the containing object. (2) A bean that receives an identity at run time. A variable by itself contains no data or program logic; it must be connected such that it receives run-time identity from a bean elsewhere in the application.

versioned edition. An edition that has been versioned and can no longer be modified.

versioning. The act of making an open edition a versioned edition; that is, making the edition read-only.

view. (1) A visual bean, such as a window, push button, or entry field. (2) A visual representation that can display and change the underlying model objects of an application. Views are both the end result of developing an application and the basic unit of composition of user interfaces. Compare with *visual bean*. Contrast with *model*.

visual bean. In the Visual Composition Editor, a bean that is visible to the end user in the graphical user interface. Compare with *view*. Contrast with *nonvisual bean*.

visual programming tool. A tool that provides a means for specifying programs graphically. Application programmers write applications by manipulating graphical representations of components.

Visual Composition Editor. In VisualAge for Java, the tool where you can create graphical user interfaces from prefabricated beans and define relationships (connections) between both visual and nonvisual beans. The Visual Composition Editor is a page in the class browser.

W

WAS. WebSphere Application Server.

WLM. Work load management.

Workbench. In VisualAge for Java, the main window from which you can manage the workspace, create and modify code, and open browsers and other tools.

workspace. The work area that contains all the code you are currently working on (that is, current editions). The workspace also contains the standard Java class libraries and other class libraries.

Index

Numerics

dynamic state   125

E
EJB
   client   51
   group
      association   62
ejbCreate
   association   72
ejbPostCreate
   association   73
enterprise network
   security   15

F
filters   18
findEntityForUpdate   165
finder
   access bean   52
   greedy   103, 108
   lazy   103
firewall   15

G
Granularity   160
granularity   123
greedy
   finder   103, 108

H
heartbeat
   dispatcher   9
high-availability   9
Home Caching   149
Home Factory   149
home interface
   access bean   52
horizontal scaling
   cloning   13
HTTP server   15
HTTP streaming   142

I
init_xx
   access bean   53
interaction
   servlet   123

inverse association maintenance   69
isolation level   159

J
JavaBean
   command   25
JNDI
   access bean   54

L
lazy
   finder   103
lazy initialization
   access bean   54
LDAP   15
linkage internal method
   association   67
load balancing
   TCP/IP   8
locating
   initial context   149

M
method-level security   47
middleware
   home grown   47
model
   cloning   14
models   48
multiple database   45
multiple protocol
   command   28
multi-valued getter   94

N
named states   125
naming context
   caching   149
no-arg constructor
   access bean   52

O
operating systems
   dispatcher   9

IBM Redbooks review

Your feedback is valued by the Redbook authors. In particular we are interested in situations where a Redbook "made the difference" in a task or problem you encountered. Using one of the following methods, **please review the Redbook, addressing value, subject matter, structure, depth and quality as appropriate.**

- Use the online **Contact us** review redbook form found at ibm.com/redbooks
- Fax this form to: USA International Access Code + 1 914 432 8264
- Send your comments in an Internet note to redbook@us.ibm.com

Document Number **Redbook Title**	SG24-5754-00 Design and Implement Servlets, JSPs, and EJBs for IBM WebSphere Application Server
Review	
What other subjects would you like to see IBM Redbooks address?	
Please rate your overall satisfaction:	O Very Good O Good O Average O Poor
Please identify yourself as belonging to one of the following groups:	O Customer O Business Partner O Solution Developer O IBM, Lotus or Tivoli Employee O None of the above
Your email address: The data you provide here may be used to provide you with information from IBM or our business partners about our products, services or activities.	O Please do not use the information collected here for future marketing or promotional contacts or other communications beyond the scope of this transaction.
Questions about IBM's privacy policy?	The following link explains how we protect your personal information. ibm.com/privacy/yourprivacy/

IBM Redbooks review

Your feedback is valued by the Redbook authors. In particular we are interested in situations where a Redbook "made the difference" in a task or problem you encountered. Using one of the following methods, **please review the Redbook, addressing value, subject matter, structure, depth and quality as appropriate.**

- Use the online **Contact us** review redbook form found at ibm.com/redbooks
- Fax this form to: USA International Access Code + 1 914 432 8264
- Send your comments in an Internet note to redbook@us.ibm.com

Document Number **Redbook Title**	SG24-5754-00 Design and Implement Servlets, JSPs, and EJBs for IBM WebSphere Application Server
Review	
What other subjects would you like to see IBM Redbooks address?	
Please rate your overall satisfaction:	O Very Good O Good O Average O Poor
Please identify yourself as belonging to one of the following groups:	O Customer O Business Partner O Solution Developer O IBM, Lotus or Tivoli Employee O None of the above
Your email address: The data you provide here may be used to provide you with information from IBM or our business partners about our products, services or activities.	O Please do not use the information collected here for future marketing or promotional contacts or other communications beyond the scope of this transaction.
Questions about IBM's privacy policy?	The following link explains how we protect your personal information. ibm.com/privacy/yourprivacy/

IBM Redbooks review

Your feedback is valued by the Redbook authors. In particular we are interested in situations where a Redbook "made the difference" in a task or problem you encountered. Using one of the following methods, **please review the Redbook, addressing value, subject matter, structure, depth and quality as appropriate.**

- Use the online **Contact us** review redbook form found at ibm.com/redbooks
- Fax this form to: USA International Access Code + 1 914 432 8264
- Send your comments in an Internet note to redbook@us.ibm.com

Document Number **Redbook Title**	SG24-5754-00 Design and Implement Servlets, JSPs, and EJBs for IBM WebSphere Application Server
Review	
What other subjects would you like to see IBM Redbooks address?	
Please rate your overall satisfaction:	O Very Good O Good O Average O Poor
Please identify yourself as belonging to one of the following groups:	O Customer O Business Partner O Solution Developer O IBM, Lotus or Tivoli Employee O None of the above
Your email address: The data you provide here may be used to provide you with information from IBM or our business partners about our products, services or activities.	O Please do not use the information collected here for future marketing or promotional contacts or other communications beyond the scope of this transaction.
Questions about IBM's privacy policy?	The following link explains how we protect your personal information. ibm.com/privacy/yourprivacy/